Wrestling Spoken Here

by

Milt Sherman

Dedication

This book is dedicated to my wife Rose Marie and our sons Michaël and Robert. Also to my high school coach Chuck Harris and my college coach John Welborn, both members of their respective state chapters of the National Wrestling Hall of Fame. I was well-coached.

ISBN 978-1-105-63586-1

CONTENTS

Arthur L. Canady H.S. Line-up

103 Justin Baker

112 Gary Newby

119 Floyd Bennett

125 Chris Farner

*130 Robbie Renfro

135 J. D. Maloney

140 Matt Ardmore

145 Artel Hardy

152 Martin Haislip

160 Terrance Ellison

171 Kevin Hopkins

189 Charles Longstrom

215 James Woodson

275 Danny Bozworth

Coach Michael Destin

Assistant Coach Moore

Team Nickname – "Pirates"
Colors – Purple & Gold
Town – Laurentville

Chapter 1 - Trying Out

"What have I got myself into now," Robbie slowly muttered under his breath. Charles Longstrom, big, loud, and one of the seniors on the team laughed and said "Hey kid, we haven't even had a tough practice yet. Coach Destin gradually makes things tougher."

"Tougher than this I don't need," Robbie thought to himself, not wanting to share that sentiment with one of the upperclassmen. Robbie Renfro was a sophomore, about 133 pounds but had a wiry strength about him. He thought of himself as a pretty tough guy for his size, at least he had until today.

Trying out for the wrestling team at Arthur L. Canady High School had seemed like a great idea when talking to his friend Matt Ardmore at lunch. Matt was an upbeat guy who obviously enjoyed competing for the wrestling team. Matt had had a winning record for the JV team last year as a ninth grader, starting at the 130 pound class, and had a good shot at the varsity 140-pound slot as a sophomore. Other wrestlers that stopped by their lunch table liked to kid with Matt, calling him “wrestling Matt” or “door Matt.”

It was Matt who had convinced Robbie to come to a few pre-season workouts. Those had been fun. Low-key. Matt had shown Robbie the basic top, bottom, and standing positions and a few moves. The workouts were a mixture of rookies and experienced athletes. During “live” wrestling, Robbie had at least held his own with the other rookies but had gotten “hammered” by the experienced wrestlers. Probably the key moment in Robbie’s decision to try out for the team was at the last pre-season workout when he took down returning 130-pound varsity starter J.D. Maloney.

While not the team's best wrestler, J.D. had been pounding Robbie in workouts up to that point. J.D. had reached for Robbie's head and gotten himself leaning forward just as Robbie had hit the double-leg takedown Matt had taught him a couple of weeks earlier. Robbie had caught both of J.D.'s legs and it was a sweet feeling when Robbie pushed his head into J.D.'s hip and realized he was off-balance and on his way down! Robbie followed-through behind for the takedown and Matt immediately let out a yell. "J.D., who's a door mat now? You look pretty flat down there on your face!"

Yes, the pre-season workouts had been mostly fun with a little soreness the next day. Team practice, Robbie was discovering, was about physical conditioning under the watchful eye of Coach Michael Destin. Practice had begun with more calisthenics then Robbie would have preferred. Some stretching was followed by a 10-minute jog in the halls. Coach Destin announced the jog by declaring "Ok guys, it's time for a little fun run!" The wrestling room at A.L. Canady H.S. was adjacent to the gym and at the end of a two-story section of the building. As a sophomore, Robbie was well aware that students shouldn't run in the halls, but that was about to change. The "fun run" sent the wrestlers down the long hallway to the cafeteria lobby. At the lobby the upperclassmen leading the run turned sharply right and began running up the stairs to the second floor. There, they turned sharply left into the second floor hallway and ran to the end of the hall and back down another set of steps to the gym lobby.

It was a tough lap! Some of the leaders seemed to have no fear, flying down the steps. Robbie was trying to keep up with Matt with some success and vainly hoped this "fun run" had ended back near the wrestling room. But no! They endured a full ten minutes of running and fighting the stairs. When Coach Destin called time, Jerry another rookie who was looking unusually pale, asked Coach to be excused and staggered toward the bathroom.

"You fellas look pretty well warmed up," beamed a smiling Coach Destin. "Let's head for the room and learn some wrestling." Strangely enough, there wasn't any "wrestling" at the first wrestling practice. At least not any "live" or full-speed wrestling. The rest of practice was spent learning and drilling moves. Robbie worked out mostly with Matt.

After practice and a shower Robbie caught a ride home with one of the upperclassmen who lived out his way. Robbie's dad sometimes joked that they lived "on the wrong side of the tracks." There was, in fact, the tracks of an old freight line two blocks from their house and they didn't exactly live in the best part of town. Theirs was a working class neighborhood of mostly one-story frame houses.

At dinner his mom asked him how practice went. Robbie acknowledged that he was tired and a little sore but he felt good about trying out for the team. In the past his teachers had frequently told him not to run in school, so Robbie was about to relate his episode of running the halls and steps when his dad asked, "You didn't have to wrestle any of them black kids did you?" Robbie simply replied, "Not today." His dad continued, "Some of them black kids may look strong but you just stay after 'em and you'll wear 'em down. Don't you lose to no black kid."

Robbie's dad had never had much of anything good to say about blacks, particularly after he'd had a couple beers which, at home, happened all too frequently. Still, when out shopping or getting the car fixed Robbie had never seen his dad have a confrontation with a black person. Seemingly, one-on-one he could relate to them as people, but as a race he held bad feelings for them somehow. His dad was a hard working guy. He got up before dawn every day to drive to his construction job and while he drank too much at home, it never affected his job. He never missed work or drank on the job. He could, however, get pretty depressed and frequently loud after he'd had a few. During warmer weather it wasn't unusual for him to fall asleep after dinner with his head on his hands on the picnic table in the back yard.

Chapter 2 – Conflict

The alarm went off and Robbie got up to start a new day. Getting up a little slower and sorer than the previous day. Still, no worse for wear; thoughts of getting to school and practice were motivating today. As he headed to the kitchen for breakfast he passed his dad who was headed for the car and work. His dad said, "Remember what I told you about those black kids. They just don't have endurance like most white kids. If you push 'em they'll wear out." With that he was off to work.

Growing up in an almost all-white neighborhood Robbie had heard such sentiments off and on, not just from his dad but from others as well. Most of the comments sounded fairly reasonable but it was difficult to separate fact from prejudice. He had heard that blacks were fast but lacked endurance. That they just wouldn't tough it out when the going got tough. That blacks just weren't as smart.

On the other hand, Robbie was watching the sports on TV one night when the Boston Marathon results were announced and it was won by a black man. 26 miles he thought, and people say they haven't got any endurance? He had seen an ESPN special on Michael Jordan and how competitive he was. Jordan didn't seem to fold in the clutch. If you mentioned that the U.S. had had a Secretary of State who was black there were those in the neighborhood who would give negative examples of blacks or other ethnic groups which sounded fairly sensible. Anyway, he hadn't figured it all out yet.

At lunch Matt sat down with him and asked, "You're sore today, aren't you?" "Not too bad," Robbie replied, "Not as bad as I'd thought." Robbie had bought a pack of M&M's on the way down the hall and asked Matt if he wanted a couple, even though he knew the answer. He poured a few on Matt's tray. A student in the hallway had been selling them as a club fund-raiser. This happened so often that Arthur L. Canady High School was jokingly referred to as A.L. "Candy." Robbie asked Matt when he'd find out if he made the team and Matt informed him that "trying out" wasn't really accurate. Coach Destin wasn't going to cut anybody that hustled and got to practice every day. That was good news.

Robbie figured he had a good chance of starting for the JV at his natural weight of 133 pounds which would put him in the 135 pound weight class behind varsity starter J.D. Maloney, who had moved up a weight since last year. At different points in practice he worked out with other wrestlers fairly close to his own weight including one of the black kids on the team, Floyd Bennett. Floyd said he weighed about 128 but planned to drop down to 119 for the varsity position. He'd started at 112 last year but had grown some.

During the second week of practice Robbie was heading down the back hall towards his first period English class when it became apparent that there was some sort of altercation in the hallway. As he got closer he could see that the black wrestler he worked out with some, Floyd, was having words, loud words, with Jake Armstrong. They had to be separated by the assistant principal and escorted down to the office. Many of the spectators were excited by the brief spectacle and a couple even yelled for one or the other to throw a punch. Neither had, though there had been some contact.

Robbie recognized Jake Armstrong, a white kid, from the back side of his own neighborhood. Jake was something of the neighborhood bully, at least with the smaller kids. He didn't mess with the "big kids" or generally with the athletes. Jake was definitely one of those in the neighborhood who didn't have much good to say about blacks in general.

At practice that afternoon he learned that both Floyd and Jake had been sent home for the day. Floyd would miss practice again tomorrow, being required to stay in "In-school Suspension" for the day and not participate in extra-curricular activities. At the end of practice Coach Destin made his usual string of announcements and then told a story relating to Floyd's situation. He pointed out that a man had the right to defend himself, but it was usually better to walk away from trouble. Floyd's situation was not only hurting himself, he said, but also hurting the team both because he was missing practice and because having a wrestler sent to the office didn't look good for the team. Coach Destin related that he had had one of his former state champions, James Whitcomb, in a similar situation a few years back. A "tough-guy" had transferred in from another school and apparently wanting to make a name for himself confronted James in a hallway during the change of classes. The troublemaker was running his mouth and trying to pick a fight. "James," said Coach Destin, "was perfectly capable of picking that guy right up in the air and slamming him down on the concrete, if he wanted to. Instead, James just smiled at the guy and walked on to class. James was a good student and didn't want to get in any trouble even if the other guy didn't care. James also had enough confidence in himself to walk away. He knew he didn't have to prove his 'manhood' to some troublemaker."

You could tell that all the team members paid close attention to the story, moral and all. Matt elbowed Robbie afterwards and said that the guys referred to this as "story time." Coach Destin, it seems, had been coaching long enough to frequently give real-life examples for almost any situation.

With practice over, the guys headed for the locker room. There was a sign above the wrestling room door which read “Go For It.” Charles Longstrum, the team’s 189-pounder, smacked the sign for good luck on the way out, as he always did. Coach Destin asked to see Robbie in his office.

Coach Destin’s office was across the hallway from the wrestling room. Screwed to the top of the door jamb was a 1”x6” board the width of the door. It looked like the carpentry class had taken a router to the board to spell out “Wrestling Spoken Here” on it. “What have I done wrong,” wondered Robbie as he stepped through the doorway. There wasn’t a lot of extra space in the office, but Coach Destin gestured for Robbie to take a seat while he sat at his desk. Coach said, “I can tell you’ve picked up a lot in your first two weeks and I like your hustle. In wrestling, if you hustle and just hang in there long enough you can become a winner. Matt tells me you plan to try out for JV 135. Is that right?" Robbie stammered out that he figured so since he weighed about 133 pounds.

Coach Destin indicated that the varsity was pretty solid with Matt at 140 and returning starter J.D. Maloney at 135 but we only had a JV kid at 130. "With a natural weight of 133 you're probably leaving practice after a good workout weighing 130 anyway. By watching what you eat some and gradually getting in better shape you could make 130 and have a shot at the varsity line up. How's that sound?" Robbie hesitated. It sounded good but as a rookie he hadn't really considered the varsity. Just last week he was just hoping to make the team.

He finally spoke, "Coach, if you think I can do it, I'm all yours!" Destin suggested that he keep eating three decent meals and just cut out the junk food. Maybe start some running. Back in the locker room Robbie was all smiles and quietly told Matt about his meeting. Matt replied, “Look, we’ve got wrestle-offs next week. Starting tomorrow let’s stay a little late each day and get you sharp.”

Chapter 3 – Wrestle-Offs

The next day Robbie and Matt stuck around after practice for an additional workout. Not that they hadn't already had a good workout. Robbie was already tired but focused on the new goal of making the varsity. The wrestling room at Canady H. S. seemed crowded during practice what with both the JV and varsity working out together but it sure looked big with just the two of them and Charles Longstrom, who was getting in some extra running. Matt said Charles was still a few pounds over 189.

Robbie had been in the wrestling room several times during his freshman year during physical education class. First for a wrestling unit, later for fitness testing, and even for volleyball a couple days when the gym was tied up for other uses. A net could be stretched across the room to recessed hooks in opposite walls. Two full 38'x38' wrestling mats spanned the floor in Canady's purple and gold school colors. The practice side of the mats were up and 18 practice circles were showing, three on each of the six sections of mat. Each of the 38' square mats was cut into three sections, each able to be rolled up and moved to the gym on match days.

Robbie and Matt got to work reviewing and practicing some of the techniques. Matt explained that while Coach Destin had shown quite a few holds and techniques in the first two weeks of practice, that most successful wrestlers ended up with just a few favorite holds that they could confidently score with. "Then why learn so many?" asked Robbie, "It's pretty confusing learning the 'single-leg takedown' right after I'd figured out the 'double-leg takedown,' or remembering not to move my left hand like I'm starting a 'switch' for a reversal, while trying the 'turn-in roll' we just learned." Matt replied, "Hey, like I'm saying, you'll figure out what offensive moves you're most comfortable with and emphasize those in practice. But you still need to know the others for defense." That made sense. Robbie had been repeatedly scored on by the varsity wrestlers with moves he was unfamiliar with. Sometimes they would kid him after a score, saying something like, "We haven't shown you that one yet, have we?"

Matt indicated that they would just drill a few of the moves Robbie was pretty natural at. So far that was the 'double-leg' takedown, the 'turn-in roll,' and the 'cross face cradle.' Midway through their drills Charles completed his run, said he thought he'd "save some for tomorrow," and headed to the locker room slapping the "Go For It" sign for good luck on the way out. Robbie and Matt finished their drills, got in a run, and headed out.

Floyd was back at practice the next day and seemed glad to be back. One of the guys had said that Floyd had a photo of Malcolm X with raised fist taped up in his locker and Jake Armstrong had walked by and said something wise about it leading to the confrontation. Neither had been willing to back down.

At the end of practice Coach Destin reminded us that for team strength it was important for every man to be at every practice. The only team rule we really needed, he said was, "Never do ***anything*** that could hurt the Arthur L. Canady wrestling team." Coach reminded us of the way former champion James Whitcomb had handled the similar situation and pointed out to Floyd that James had also been a young, black athlete but had just thought through the situation better. When Coach Destin dismissed the team, Martin the 152-pounder kidded Floyd saying, "Yeah, we know you want to win…'by any means necessary!'" A few of the wrestlers chuckled, recognizing the play-on-words of a Malcolm X quote.

After practice that day, Coach Destin stuck around the room too, running Floyd through a make-up workout. He complimented Robbie and Matt on their dedication and said it would pay off. Today Matt suggested some strategy to Robbie. He mentioned that Jamie Byrd, Robbie's opponent in the wrestle-offs was more experienced, having had mixed results at the JV level last year, but was probably less athletic than Robbie. Jamie's balance, Matt said, just wasn't that good and as a result he was a "sucker" for a 'turn-in roll.' The roll is executed by the bottom wrestler sitting-out and then, while controlling the top man's wrist, quickly turning to the left and rolling the top man over to his back. Executed correctly it could lead to a pin or at least a 4-point move, two points for the reversal and two points for a near fall.

Robbie and Matt continued their extra workouts each afternoon and Robbie started doing some push-ups and sit-ups each morning before breakfast. Tuesday arrived and Robbie found "wrestle-off day" to be something of a 3-ring circus. One of the three-piece competition mats had been flipped over exposing a ten-foot circle and starting lines inside the 28-foot out-of-bounds circle. There was also a menacing Pirate painted in the center, the school's mascot.

Wrestle-offs were to be conducted during the entire practice on the competition mat and rather than have the entire JV and varsity sitting around and waiting their turn, the JV coach would run about half the team through drills on the other mat while a couple of the seniors had several teammates out running the halls or exercising in the gym lobby. Coach Destin apparently didn't believe in a lot of sitting around.

Robbie and Matt were drilling moves while the 103-pounders wrestled-off and Robbie mentioned how active Coach Destin managed to keep the whole team. Matt replied, “Right. He must think sitting around causes cancer. He’s Michael Destin, that’s M. D., so sometimes we call him the ‘wrestling doctor.’ Anyway, he’s not going to let anybody get lazy from sitting around. Besides, losing can be like a cancer, it spreads.”

Robbie really hadn’t had time to get nervous about his wrestle-off with Jamie since he’d been so busy drilling with Matt. He started to feel some “butterflies,” though, when he stepped into the 28-foot circle and put on the green ankle band; Jamie was wearing the red one. The wrestle-offs were intended to be as much like a real match as possible. The team manager and one of the seniors were keeping the time and score over against the wall. The match would be six minutes in length divided into 3 two-minute periods unless a pin occurred which would end the match.

Robbie and Jamie stepped to the starting lines, shook hands and Coach Destin blew the whistle to start the action. The wrestlers tied up and worked for inside control with their hands. Robbie knew he wanted the win, so without much of a set-up, shot his 'double-leg' takedown which Jamie blocked readily as if he knew it was coming. Next, Jamie snapped Robbie's head down and spun behind for control. Coach Destin declared, "Two, takedown."

Surprised by the suddenness of the score, Robbie hesitated but Jamie didn't. Robbie felt himself broken down to his stomach with Jamie's 'tight-waist arm-chop' and his trying for a 'half nelson.' Robbie would have none of that and, keeping his elbows in, worked back up to his knees and tried to throw a 'switch' but Jamie saw it coming and hit a ‘shoulder-drive’ and forced Robbie back to his stomach. “Eating mat” was not what Robbie had in mind so he worked back up to his knees and, remembering Matt’s coaching, sat-out and hit his ‘turn-in roll.’ Jamie’s suspect balance came into play and over he went to his back. Coach Destin signaled “Two, reversal.” Robbie was so surprised by the sudden turn of events that he released Jamie’s wrist allowing him to fight back to his stomach. No near fall, so the score was locked at 2-2 as the first period ended.

Robbie started on top for the second period and “rode” Jamie pretty well with his ‘shoelace and cross-face’ ride while attempting to lock him up in a ‘cradle’ pinning combination. Halfway through the period they went out of bounds giving Jamie a fresh start from bottom. Wanting nothing to do with Robbie’s cross-face anymore, Jamie immediately hit a ‘stand-up’ on the whistle and was able to turn his hips effectively for an escape. Coach Destin called out, “One, escape.” The period ended with Jamie up 3-2.

Robbie started on the bottom in the third and final period with thoughts of another two point reversal with his roll. Jamie’s experience was paying off, however, and he rode Robbie carefully nursing his 3-2 lead. As Coach Destin had recognized after earlier practices, Robbie ***would*** hustle and late in the period Robbie caught Jamie out of position and again rolled him to his back. Coach Destin declared, “Two, reversal” but this time Robbie maintained control of Jamie’s wrist and held him on his back for a near fall before Jamie managed to bridge over to his stomach. With the near fall points Robbie was the winner 6-3. Robbie and Jamie again shook hands and Coach Destin raised Robbie’s arm in victory. It was just a wrestle-off against a teammate but for Robbie it felt good. Real good.

After practice Coach Destin pointed out to Robbie that his 'double-leg' takedown had failed because he really hadn't set it up and he could work on that. "You won on hustle, though," he said, "and I like that."

Chapter 4 – The Scrimmage

As the end of the third week of practice approached, the wrestlers were looking forward to Friday night's scrimmage against the Eagles of Thomas Edison H. S. over in the next county. Wrestling against the same people every day was getting a little old, and they were each other's teammates anyway. Putting on the Pirate purple and gold for the first time was on every athlete's mind, even if it was just a scrimmage.

The team met in the wrestling room after school, ready to go. Coach Destin had a few words to say about "bus decorum" and how we were representing our high school and should wrestle tough but leave our hosts a positive impression. Coach Destin pointed out that with the level of experience on this year's team that we should do well, but since it was a scrimmage no official team score would be kept. Martin Haislip, a senior 152-pounder, and one of the black kids on the team chirped in with, "So you feel it's our 'destiny' to win, Coach?" Several of the returning wrestlers chuckled and the Coach answered with a smile, "Something like that, Martin." Matt explained to him that this was a running joke on the team, a play on words with the Coach's name. One of the wrestlers would joke, "It's your destiny," and a teammate would add, "No, it's just Coach Destin talking again."

As they got on the bus the upperclassmen called the back seats. Robbie sat with Matt near the middle of the bus and most of the JV got stuck with the coaches up near the front. A few of the guys sat sideways playing cards while one or two pulled out a book to actually use their time wisely, often to taunts of, "Don't get too smart before we get to Edison H. S."

Since it was a scrimmage, Edison H. S. had set up two mats in the gym and there was a referee for each. In fact, there were several referees. Coach Destin explained that it was a scrimmage for the wrestlers, coaches, and referees. We should go hard but no one was expected to be in mid-season form, including the officials. Both mats ran simultaneously with the JV on one and the varsity on the other. The aim was to get a match for every wrestler on both teams.

Robbie was told that he would have the fifth match on the varsity mat. It would be against a black fellow named Queen he'd seen at weigh-in. His teammate Floyd said, "I beat him last year but he's moved up a couple weights. Keep hustling and you can get him." Experience was to win the match, though. Robbie hustled but couldn't quite finish his scoring attempts before getting countered. In the meantime Queen managed a takedown and a reversal for a 4-0 win. So much for what his dad had said about black kids quitting if you pushed them!

The team had done better than Robbie, at least at most weights. Floyd, Matt, Martin, and Charles had pinned their Edison Eagle opponents while several other Pirates had won decisions. There had been no official team score but it was clear that A. L. Canady had had the upper hand. As for Robbie, as Matt said to him after the match, "Look, Edison comes to our place next month and you can beat him on our mat." "I hope so," said Robbie but after being shut out he didn't feel too confident about it.

The team tumbled back onto the bus for the trip back to school. As the bus pulled out of the gym parking lot onto the access road around to the front of the school, a noticeable change could be seen. When the team arrived for weigh-in there was hardly a car in front of the school. Now, apparently there was a concert or some other well-attended event taking place, and the front of the school was absolutely packed with cars. Cars were also parallel parked on both sides of the curving access road, which was not designed for that purpose. As a result the bus could scarcely squeeze through the gauntlet of automobiles.

If anything, the available space for the bus was becoming even more constricted as the bus progressed. The main road in front of the school was visible but apparently was going to be a tough place to get to. Talk on the bus had shifted from the just-completed match to the maze of cars we now found ourselves in. Frustrated, Coach Destin opened the bus door and had his assistant, Coach Moore walk in front of the bus, first gesturing to edge the bus slightly left or slightly right. This worked, but slowly, as the bus progressed towards the street with only one curve left to negotiate on the access road and then on to McDonald's!

Unfortunately, just up ahead a couple of poorly parked vehicles stuck out just far enough that Hercules could not have squeezed the bus through. Coach Destin stopped the bus. He stepped out himself to survey the scene, shook his head, conversed apparently without success with his assistant coach, both gesturing with their hands, and got back on the bus. There was no way to take that bus forward, and Richard Petty couldn't have backed it out without sideswiping a dozen cars.

Coach Destin then surprised the team by ordering the starters in the five heaviest weight classes to step outside. "Bozworth, Woodson, Longstrom, Hopkins, and Ellison," he called. No one knew what he had in mind, but tired of being stuck on the bus most of the team was immediately on its feet volunteering for service. Coach Destin insisted five was enough and instructed the rest to stay on the bus. Faces were soon pressed against the bus windows to follow the action.

What happened next was all around school the next day by first bell. One of the cars jutting out into our path was a Toyota Camry and Coach Destin instructed the five to lift its front bumper and place its right front wheel up onto the curb. The "weight-lifters" then performed the same feat of strength on the rear bumper and once more from front and back.

Presto! The five had cleared enough roadway for the bus to pass through. Soon, Coach Destin was back in the driver's seat and like Harry Houdini had made an amazing escape from impending doom.

Chapter 5 – Back to Work

"Today is a good day for a Saturday," Robbie thought the next morning. He still wasn't too happy about the shut-out loss but maybe, like Matt had said, he could beat him next time. One thing good about sports was that there was almost always another chance. Robbie went next door to Al Crawford's house and they shot some baskets in the driveway.

Halfway through a game of one-on-one Jake Armstrong and two of his cronies walked by smoking cigarettes. One of them, the smaller of the three, was wearing a rebel flag t-shirt emblazoned with "Hell No, I Won't Forget!" Seeing the game in progress, Jake yelled over, "Hey Robbie, that darkie Floyd the wrestler ain't no friend of yours is he? I hear you're out for the team." Jake's friends chuckled.

This put Robbie on the spot. He wasn't fond of Jake, in fact he thought that he was a pain in the butt, but he'd known him for years. They had played in a lot of pick-up games around the neighborhood. For whatever reason, Robbie had never been one of the many that Jake bullied around. Floyd, he'd really just met but they were teammates now and sometimes workout partners. Robbie answered back, "Jake, Floyd's okay, you just don't know him very well."

To the amusement of his friends, Jake called back, "Floyd better watch his butt or he's going to get to know my fist real well!" Al looked a little nervous. He knew these guys played rough sometimes. Robbie replied, "I wouldn't mess with Floyd. He's been wrestling for a few years and he can take care of himself." "Shoot Robbie," said Jake, "Floyd's even smaller than you are. I'd crush him and you know it!" Not wanting to aggravate

Jake too much, Robbie gave a little ground, but not too much saying, "You might Jake if you hit him with a clean shot, but if Floyd got under you with his 'double-leg' takedown he could throw you on your ear. I know. I've been on the receiving end."

"That's about right," said Jake, "I'll drop him right on his 'receiving end!'" Jake's friends laughed again and they continued down the street, taking another drag on their cigarettes.

After warm-up at practice on Monday, Coach Destin was holding his clipboard in his hand and he had the team members each sit with a partner. He had taken notes at the scrimmage Friday night and had several mistakes, he said, we needed to improve on. Thinking back to Friday night, Robbie recalled what a difference in personalities the coaches seemed to display during the competition despite the fact that both were known to run successful programs.

The Edison H. S. coach was loud and mobile. He yelled a lot at both his wrestlers and the officials, frequently while storming back and forth in front of the bench. Coach Destin, conversely, almost never left his seat. And while he occasionally yelled encouragement to his wrestlers, he never seemed to yell at the official. In the gym, the clipboard had been leaning against the side of Coach Destin's chair and every few minutes he had picked it up, hurriedly jotted a few notes and then set it back down.

As the coach ran down through a couple pages of notes with the team Robbie came to realize they were divided into two categories, individual and team. In cases in which an individual seemed to be repeating a particular mistake like a poor stance or an incorrect technique, Coach Destin would grab one of the upperclassmen as a "dummy" and demonstrate the necessary correction. He then sent the individual over in a corner to practice that specific correction with Coach Moore or a teammate.

When the Coach felt the mistake was a general one that many of the team members had had a problem with, he then drilled the entire team on the correction. Matt noted to Robbie, "I hear this is why Coach Destin has never had a losing season. We all make mistakes. Destin makes sure that you don't keep making the same ones over and over and losing matches because of it. 'Doctor' Destin cures all mistakes."

When Robbie's turn came, Coach Destin said that he had hustled and that was the most important thing he was looking for in a rookie. His biggest mistake was just not "setting up" his 'double-leg' takedown and he sent Robbie over to Coach Moore to work on it. Set-ups are fakes or feints to make a move work better. Robbie had been shown several set-ups, but having seen so many new things in a short time, as a rookie he was too confused to have caught on to one. Coach Moore said, “Look, you like to make contact, let’s review the ‘snap and go.’” Coach Moore demonstrated the ‘snap and go’ set-up in which the offensive wrestler attempts to snap his opponent’s head and shoulder down. His opponent reacts by popping his head back up, which creates an opening for the ‘double-leg’ takedown. After several repetitions Coach Moore told Robbie to continue practicing the set-up in future workouts and Robbie sat back down with Matt.

At the end of practice Coach Destin mentioned that the team bus had driven past Israel Smith’s trailer Friday night on the way to Edison H.S. Robbie had no idea who Israel Smith might be and Matt elbowed him and whispered, “Story time.” “You seniors would remember Israel placing third in the State Tournament," Coach continued. "For you younger guys, Israel lived in a trailer out in the country. It's the last trailer you pass before you cross over the county line. Israel's folks didn't have much, but they did make sure they got him home from football and wrestling practice every night despite the long drive. Unlike many of your families they really couldn't afford an extra car. The Sunday afternoon that we got back from the State Tournament," Coach Destin continued, "Israel used the phone in my office to call home for a ride as he usually did. His dad told him his car was outside. Israel disagreed saying he'd just come in and the family car wasn't out there. His dad then told Israel that the Camaro parked out in front was his and the keys were under the floor mat. Well, it may have been a used car, but believe me Israel was one happy fellow," said Coach. "I've always felt," Coach continued, "that Israel was a good example of a hard working person that things worked out well for. There may not be a Camaro in it for you, but if you hang in there tough, good things will happen."

Chapter 6 – Conflict Returns

On purpose, Robbie got to English class a bit earlier than usual the next day. He wanted some time to review for the scheduled test. Strangely though, when the bell rang his teacher, Mr. Long, wasn't there yet. This was a particular surprise since Mr. Long was constantly reminding the class of the importance of promptness, often saying, "A good work ethic starts with being on time." Also, just as the bell rang several students rushed in excitedly declaring that there was a fight down the hall and they couldn't get by. Few details were available but Robbie had a bad feeling about it when he heard it involved a white and a black. A few minutes later Mr. Long showed up, announcing as he walked through the door, "Clear your desks and get ready for the test."

By lunch time Robbie had heard, as he feared, that Floyd and Jake Armstrong had been the two involved and that Jake had been badly hurt. That was something of a surprise since Jake must outweigh Floyd by fifty pounds! About the time Matt sat down with Robbie they were surprised to see Floyd walk into the cafeteria. They figured him to have been sent home by then, probably for several days. They called Floyd over to their table and asked him to sit down and fill them in on what happened. "Hey 'Door Matt,' Robbie" he said as he sat down.

Floyd said that he remembered what Coach had said about not hurting the team by getting suspended, "but here comes that redneck Jake running his mouth again. No way I was going to miss the season opener Friday night with you guys," said Floyd. "Jake pointed to the picture of Malcolm X in my locker and says that's he's no good and just wanted to burn down everything and I'm trying to tell him that that's not so, I just like him because he stood up for black people."

I'm trying to tell Jake to just leave me alone. I don't want no trouble," Floyd said, "Then his buddies behind him got into it. One of them yells, 'Get him Jake!' and the other tells him to 'Lay him out' or something," said Floyd. "Anyway," he continued, "maybe he just couldn't back off with his buddies egging him on and for no good reason he takes a swing right at my head. I don't know if it was the wrestling reflexes kicking in or just trying to stay alive but I ducked the punch," said Floyd. "Immediately there was this loud bang and Jake screamed. You know I was just trying to get my Science book out of my locker when these three goons showed up and the locker was still open. Anyway," he continued, "Jake's fist must have hit the front corner of the locker where the door would shut. You could hear the bones break. It was nasty!"

"Serves him right," said Matt. "Yeah, serves him right," said Floyd, "but I'm glad it wasn't my hand! Anyway, I got run down to the office again and I'm figuring I'm in big trouble when Mr. Long the English teacher walks in. He was down there helping in the hallway after it happened. He said he saw the whole thing and that it wasn't my fault so I'm still a free man!" "Way to go Mr. Long," said Robbie.

After school Floyd had trouble getting from the locker room to the wrestling room since so many of the team members had heard about Jake's hand and wanted the details. Danny Bozworth, the team's heavyweight and one of the seniors cleared the locker room out, declaring, "Let's move it guys, the season opener's Friday night!" Nobody argued with the 260 pound heavyweight.

Working mostly with Matt and Floyd during practice, Robbie put special emphasis on the 'snap and go' set-up. He already felt pretty natural shooting the 'double-leg.' Adding the set-up would hopefully help him begin to score on some of the experienced wrestlers. Realizing he might be wrestling-off Jamie again in the future he put some time in on his 'turn-in roll' as well.

Coach Destin began drilling the team on the 'cross-face cradle' and Robbie was taking turns with Matt. In quick succession, Coach was barking out, "Step 1 shoelace and waist. Step 2 cross-face. Step 3 drive the head to the knee." At that point Coach Moore put his hand on Robbie's shoulder and said, "Hold it right there. I think I see why you can't seem to lock this up during a match. You're not driving the head toward the knee with your leg power. You're trying to 'muscle him.'" "Now," Coach Moore continued, "you've got the shoelace and cross-face right. Your left foot needs to about step on Matt's left hand. If you don't step out in front you can't get enough pressure."

Robbie stepped around further as instructed and Coach Moore said, "Now with your foot out in front you can drive Matt's head back to his knee. Make him kiss his knee," he joked. Matt didn't 'kiss his knee' but by driving Matt's head to the knee he could now easily lock up the cradle pinning combination. "That's right," said Coach Moore, "now rock the cradle and roll him to his back. That's why it's called a cradle." Robbie had Matt planted on both shoulders and he thought to himself, "I'd sure like to get this on somebody Friday night."

Coach Destin sat the team down at the end of practice and went over the week's schedule which would include wrestle-offs again and Friday night's season opener at Stark Central H. S. With a sly grin, Coach pointed out that Stark Central had a lot of returning starters and that was "just a Stark reality." Many groans were heard as the team reacted to the obvious pun. Coach Destin then praised Floyd for the way he had handled himself during that morning's conflict.

"I taught Jake Armstrong when he was in the ninth grade," said Coach Destin, "but I really don't know for a fact whether his problems with Floyd are due to racial prejudice or just part of his usual 'tough-guy' act. But I will say this. In my opinion high school sports are the best thing our society has to overcome racial prejudice," he said. "I say that," he went on, "because on a team you <u>have</u> to get along in order to be successful. Working out with people on your own team and competing against others also disproves a lot of the negative stereotypes and sorry jokes that most of us grow up with. Through athletics you come to realize that good people come in all shapes, sizes, and colors."

Practice ended on a serious note and Robbie found himself thinking about his father and why he said such prejudiced things. Was that just the climate that he'd grown up with? Robbie didn't know. With wrestle-offs coming up, Robbie and Matt stuck around for several minutes to drill their favorite moves and get in a run.

Chapter 7 – Ride 'em Cowboys

Robbie found himself daydreaming in class a couple times the next day about the wrestle-offs. He realized that while his opponent Jamie Byrd wasn't a great athlete, that he still had at least a year of experience on Robbie. The only move he had actually scored with against Jamie last time was the 'roll' and what if Jamie figured out a way to stop it? Robbie figured he'd better get his mind back on his schoolwork since a 'double-leg' takedown scored no points in either English or Geometry class. But then, being able to conjugate a verb won't help me very much against Jamie this afternoon, he thought.

Just after Robbie walked into the wrestling room for practice that afternoon he saw their 103-pounder Justin Baker sail across the room and jump on heavyweight Danny Bozworth. Practice hadn't started yet and Danny had been lying on his stomach talking to Charles Longstrom. "Get lost you ugly flea!" shouted Danny just as Justin locked an illegal headlock on Danny.

The upper weights looked upon Justin as a likable pest. He was an athletic small guy and won a lot of matches but always found fun in picking on the big boys. Danny rose to his feet with Justin still clinging to his head. Danny peeled off the belligerent flea and tossed him against the padded wall declaring, "Die, flea!" Justin laughed it off and sprinted to the opposite side of the room and the apparent protection of the other lightweights. Part of the fun of high school sports is the opportunity to kid around some.

Robbie didn't remember any instructions from Coach Destin on just where in the room to practice, but the lightweights always seemed to practice in the circles closest to the doors and the big guys in the back. Maybe the small guys wanted to avoid being crushed by falling heavyweights.

Robbie was nervous as his wrestle-off approached even though he had won the first time. He felt he was a little quicker and stronger than Jamie and hoped he was closing the gap in experience. When the time came for Coach Destin to blow his whistle and start the match the two wrestlers worked left and right trying for an advantage. Jamie took the first takedown shot and Robbie was almost surprised that he easily stopped the shot by popping Jamie's shoulders with his hands and hopping back as the team often practiced. "Hands" was the second of Coach Destin's "Five H's of takedown defense" that they drilled daily.

The first H was "Head." If your head blocked your opponent's shoulder as he attempted a shot, then you've stopped the shot. The second H was "Hands," blocking the opponent's chest or shoulders to stop him. The third H was "Hips." The hips, Coach said, were the strongest part of the body so even a good takedown shot could be blocked with the hips, particularly if you hooked a "whizzer," over-hooking your opponent's arm. The fourth H was "Hip-heist," which allowed a wrestler knocked even to his butt a chance to fight back to a neutral position. The fifth H was "Oh hell!" in which the shot was so good that you'd better just turn to your stomach and fight back later to get the two points back.

Still neutral and facing each other on their feet, Robbie snapped Jamie's head down and immediately shot under him for a 'double-leg' takedown. The set-up worked like a charm and Coach Destin called, "Two, takedown." Robbie rode him out for a 2-0 lead at the end of the first period. Robbie took bottom at the beginning of the second period and was surprised that Jamie just let him go. "One point, escape," called out Coach Destin. Apparently Jamie didn't want to chance getting rolled to his back again and felt safer going for takedowns. That strategy didn't work since Robbie scored another takedown late in the period to go up 5-0.

Robbie had top position in the third period and rode Jamie effectively often going for the 'cross-face cradle' unsuccessfully. Late in the period Jamie seemed to be tiring more than he and Robbie stepped out to the front, drove Jamie's head to his knee and finally locked up a 'cradle.' Robbie had him almost pinned as time ran out and scored a two-point near fall for a 7-0 win. An impressive improvement from the previous week. They shook hands and Coach raised Robbie's hand in victory. Jamie, despondently, walked out of the room for a drink of water.

Matt patted Robbie on the back and told him how much improvement he was seeing, saying "Our extra workouts are paying off. Remember your last match with Jamie when you couldn't 'buy' a takedown." Matt's back-up didn't even want to challenge him after getting "hammered" in the previous week's match. Soon it was their turn to get into the running and drilling groups.

During announcements at the end of practice Coach Destin mentioned that the difference between the team winning or losing against Stark H. S. this Friday night could well be which team scored the most pins, since a decision (winning by points) scored three points for the team as compared to six for a pin. "And remember what the cowboys say," he continued, "there ain't a horse that can't be rode, or a cowboy can't be throwed." Robbie looked at Matt and said, "Where does he come up with this stuff?" Matt just smiled. "For a wrestler that saying means a lot," Coach continued. "If you're the top wrestler then if you can ride your 'horse' you have a chance to both wear him down and possibly pin him. When you're the bottom man, however, it's your job to throw that cowboy and score some points."

Some days Coach Destin would throw in a change-of-pace activity and today he said, "Let's finish up with a push-up sit-up ladder from seven and a log run." The returning wrestlers immediately knew what he was talking about and good-naturedly starting lining up on their stomachs in a big circle around the room. Robbie lined up next to Matt. With their feet near the walls, all the wrestlers could see each other. One of the seniors yelled out, "Seven push-ups! Everybody ready?" Everybody yelled, "Ready!" The senior began calling out "Up…Up…Up!" and at each "Up" everybody did a push-up and called out the numbers until they got to seven. The wrestler next to the senior then barked out, "Seven sit-ups! Everybody ready?" Everybody yelled, "Ready!" and did their sit-ups on command.

The drill continued down through 6, 5, 4, 3, 2, and 1. At 1 push-up everyone (that could) pushed up so hard that they could clap their hands before hitting the mat.

The log run followed immediately. First the seniors got the team, still on their stomachs, slapping the mat in unison with both hands in a loud, rhythmic Indian war drum beat. A senior then got up and ran through the big circle of bodies, running fast but carefully stepping between, not on, the wrestlers. As soon as the senior started his run, the first man he stepped over got up and chased him, also stepping over each wrestler. On the circle moved with each prone wrestler getting up and giving chase as soon as he was stepped over. After a quick lap the lead wrestler dived back to his original spot followed by the others in quick succession. A total of two laps around the circle of wrestlers were made all the while with those still on their stomachs slapping out the tom-tom beat. During Danny's turns the smaller wrestlers were pleading with the 260-pounder not to slip and fall on them! After completion of the second lap, the senior yelled "1, 2, 3" for the last slaps of the mat and practice broke up on a light moment.

Chapter 8 – To Quit Or Not To Quit (That is the question.)

The next day Robbie was running a few minutes late to practice after getting some help from his Geometry teacher. His teacher, Mr. Lloyd, had kidded him saying, "I thought wrestlers knew all the angles!" The hinge on the locker room door creaked as he entered the locker room and Robbie immediately heard a muffled shout from the back row of lockers, "Help! Get me outta here!" Moving to the back of the locker room, he heard the voice continue, "I'm in here. I'm in here!" but Robbie saw no one. He could hear the voice of 103-pounder Justin Baker, though, and following the voice soon saw Justin's eyes through a slot in a locker.

Robbie laughed and asked, "What happened, Justin?" though he had a good idea. "Get me outta here! said Justin, "Danny and Charles stuck me in here and said they had to teach me a lesson." Robbie released the "prisoner" joking, "Maybe I should have left you in there. I don't want to get on the bad side of anyone who weighs 260 pounds!" "Hey," said Justin, "we lightweights got to stick together." Justin immediately headed to the wrestling room to be met with laughs and catcalls. Everybody except the coaches knew why Justin was late.

Coach Destin always checked roll while the seniors ran warm-up and he noticed that Jamie Byrd was missing and he said, "Anybody see Jamie?" One of the other JV wrestlers answered, "He said he was quitting, Coach." Coach Destin shook his head and said, "Quitting is never the answer, gentlemen."

At the end of practice Coach said he was going to stop by and see Jamie on his way home. Quitting, he said, didn't solve any problems and it was habit-forming. "Let me give you guys the example of Charles Hardy," he said. "Charles came out for the team as a ninth grader several years back. He'd never wrestled before but had a couple friends on the team. We ended up having to use Charles in the varsity line-up because he was the only man we had at that weight," said Coach. "As a ninth grader with no experience having to compete for the varsity he got beat almost every match and was really having no fun. One day he went home and told his dad he was fed up and was quitting the team. The Hardy family didn't have much financially but they did have good parenting," Destin continued. "His father told him 'Look boy, I didn't raise no quitter. Now you get back out there and finish what you started.'"

"Charles didn't particularly like it," said Coach, "but he did what his dad told him, figuring to finish the season and that would be it for wrestling. The next winter, though, his friends came back out for the team and Charles decided to give it a second chance. He was glad he did. He won the Conference Championship as a sophomore after that first losing season. His senior year, Charles placed third in the State Championships. He never would have done any of that if he hadn't had a father that 'didn't raise no quitter.'"

The student body at Arthur L. Canady H. S. came from a wide variety of backgrounds. The school was roughly 40% black and 55% white while also having a smaller percentage of Latinos and Asian-Americans. There were some nice affluent subdivisions but also some poverty as indicated by several trailer parks. In the outlying areas there were some impressively large houses, but also some which could best be described as shacks.

Jamie Byrd's home was run-down and was not much better than a shack. Coach Destin had occasionally given him a ride home and he headed there after practice. It didn't matter much during the winter but he could see that several of the window screens were torn. Jamie's little brother, a cute little kid about eight years old answered the door and went to get Jamie, yelling as he went, "Jamie, your coach is here!" As Jamie got to the door his little brother was right behind him peeking around at Coach Destin.

Jamie's chin hung down close to his chest as Coach said, "Jamie we missed you at practice today, what's up?" Jamie answered, "It's just not any fun this year." "Does that have to do with the fact that you've lost two wrestle-offs in a row?" asked Coach. "Coach, I was JV all last year and now a rookie's beating me. I'm just not getting any better." "Jamie," said the coach, "first of all, both the coaches and athletes are happy to have you on the team. Second of all, life's a two-way street. The coaching staff has promised to stick by you all season and help you improve, which we believe you will do. Conversely, you promised when you made the team to stick it out for the season and support your teammates. Now the question is, are you going to handle your responsibilities like a man?" At this point Jamie's little brother poked his head out a little further and said, "Be a man, Jamie!" Jamie bit his lip and then said, "I'll be back out there tomorrow, Coach." "That's a good decision, Jamie, we'll be glad to have you back," Destin replied.

Chapter 9 – Stark Reality

The day before the Stark H.S. match, Robbie was reading the team's schedule on the bulletin board in the wrestling room just before practice started and asked Matt, "What's the D.C. Quad?" "Didn't you know about that," replied Matt, "That's the weekend we go to Washington D.C. for three matches." "Wow!" said Robbie, "I had seen it on the schedule but didn't know what it meant. What's a quad?" Matt explained that a quad involved four teams on two mats. It was a round-robin event in which each team would wrestle the other three. "Man, that is so cool," replied Robbie, "I've never been to Washington D.C. before. Our family doesn't travel much." At that point Charles and Danny yelled for the wrestlers to line up for warm-up.

Coach Destin announced that with the season opener tomorrow that the emphasis would be on getting sharp for the match. Today was different.

They had been doing some "live" wrestling every day in practice but the day before the match was drill, drill, drill. "Live" wrestling was more fun. Usually they got in some matches against teammates or wrestled in 3-somes. In 3-somes, one man caught his breath and refereed the other two before taking his own turn in "live" wrestling. Drill was methodically practicing moves and Robbie thought they must have practiced every move and counter they had learned, and that was quite a few.

Toward the end of practice, Coach said that since they hadn't gotten any matches in, that for a change-of-pace they would finish up with some Sumo wrestling. Danny and a few others immediately cried out "All right!" Robbie didn't know anything about Sumo wrestling but he could see how their big, chunky heavyweight would like it.

Coach Destin quickly went over the basic rules. Three or four wrestlers of about the same size would take turns going at it with the winner staying in and taking on a new challenger. The basic rules were simple. The two wrestlers squatted Sumo-style facing each other in their ten-foot practice circle. When the extra guy in their group yelled "Go" they then tried to knock down their opponent or drive him out of the circle. Robbie got into a group with Matt, the team's 125-pounder Chris Farner, and the 135-pounder J.D. Maloney.

Being in unfamiliar territory Robbie was slow to volunteer to go first, but no worry as Matt and J.D. jumped into the circle and squared off with each other. Chris called "Go" and the two began hand-fighting and shoving. Matt, being a little bit bigger, managed to shove J.D. out of the circle and Chris yelled "Out!" indicating a win for Matt. Matt looked at Robbie and said, "Your turn, big boy!"

Robbie squared off with Matt but being inexperienced at Sumo was soon shoved out. It was Chris' turn next. Red-headed Chris was the smallest of their group but probably the quickest.

J.D. said "Go" for the Chris-Matt match-up. Matt immediately drove forward into the smaller Chris for an apparent fast win but Chris surprised him by side-stepping and snapping Matt's head down. Matt lunged forward and caught his balance but not before stepping outside of the ten-foot practice circle. J.D. called "Out!" Matt shook his head and smiled at Chris saying, "You suckered me on that one, carrot-top." Chris replied, "Better luck next time Matt-man." He then looked at Robbie and said, "Your turn, rookie." Robbie cautiously stepped into the circle with Chris. When J.D. called "Go" Robbie avoided trying the headlong rush that Chris had side-stepped and came in slower. Being a little bigger and stronger than Chris, Robbie held his own and eventually shoved Chris over the line for a win. Robbie thought to himself, "This is kinda fun but the real match is tomorrow night."

The next day both the JV and varsity were set for the trip to Stark Central H.S. The team members checked weight after school and a couple guys were in the wrestling room trying to run a little weight off. Justin and Kevin were both about a half pound over-weight, he heard. A couple others were playing video games while most just talked. The 160-pounder Terrance Ellison was reading a school copy of Beowulf for English class when Martin, his usual workout partner walked by and said, "Terrance, you reading again? You must be smarter than you look." "That's right," replied Terrance, "and I'm way, way smarter than <u>you</u> look!" That got a few chuckles from those nearby.

The match at Stark H. S. was what would be common during the season, a JV/varsity doubleheader. There was one competition mat in the gym and the 14 JV wrestlers competed first. It was a hard-fought match with the Canady H.S. team prevailing by several points. While watching the JV, Robbie thought to himself that it was the first time he'd seen an actual <u>JV</u> match and that he'd be wrestling for the <u>varsity</u> that night.

For the varsity, Stark's 103-pounder was just no match for Justin and the Pirate pinned him early in the second period for a 6-0 team lead. Gary lost at 112 before Floyd and Chris won the next two for the Pirates and a 12-3 team lead as Robbie stepped on the mat at 130. Just before the match, Coach Destin had patted him on the back and said, "Look everybody's a little nervous before a match. You're a tough kid, just go get him!" Despite some "butterflies," Robbie was set to do just that when the referee blew the whistle to start the match.

The two wrestlers sparred for several seconds before Robbie took the first shot. His opponent blocked the shot but Robbie hustled back to his feet and the two wrestlers tied up. Robbie felt his opponent pop him on the back of his head and then shoot under him. The next thing Robbie knew, he was doing a forward roll onto his back and trying to fight back to his stomach. Robbie was unfamiliar with the 'fireman's carry' takedown his opponent had shot. His opponent had already locked Robbie's upper arm by the time he had popped Robbie's head. He then shot in hooking the inside of Robbie's leg and rolled him over. Robbie first heard the referee sound out, "Two takedown" and then call "Two near fall" as Robbie bridged over to his stomach.

Here he was in his first real varsity match and already down 4-0! Robbie fought back up to his knees and eventually earned an escape before the end of the period. He glanced up at the scoreboard and saw the 4-1 score. Robbie started down in the second period. He "ate mat" most of the next minute as his more experienced opponent broke him down and unsuccessfully tried to turn Robbie over, first with a 'half nelson' and later with an 'arm bar.' The wrestlers then went out-of-bounds and after the fresh start Robbie hit a 'switch' for a reversal. In a 'switch' the bottom man sits out to his right side and leans on his opponent while levering the top man's leg with his right arm. The ref called "Two reversal" which closed the gap down to 4-3.

Robbie's opponent managed to escape before time was called and they went into the third period with the Stark H.S. wrestler winning 5-3. Robbie started on top in the third period knowing he needed a near fall or pin to gain the win. "Pin to win" was an expression Coach Destin frequently used. Robbie was "psyched up" for the win and frequently tried to lock up his 'cross-face cradle' but his opponent was wrestling very cautiously and stayed out of trouble. Finally, with twenty seconds left, Robbie forced his opponent's head to his knee and locked up the cradle. Sensing victory within his grasp, Robbie made every effort to "rock the cradle" but his opponent was squared off on his knees and just as determined ***not*** to go to his back. Time expired.

Both wrestlers got to their feet, shook hands, said "good match" and headed for their benches. The Stark H.S. wrestler with a big smile on his face and his hands in the air, Robbie staring at the mat and biting his lip. The thrill of victory and the agony of defeat. The team stood up as they did after every match. Coach Destin said, "Good hustle, Robbie." Several of the guys patted him on the back.

Coach Moore walked up behind Robbie, who was now sitting on the team bench, and locked him in a playful headlock saying, “That’s what I like, Robbie. You’re locking that cradle up like I said. Now next week we ‘do the bump.’” As Coach Moore moved back down the bench Robbie looked at Floyd who was sitting next to him and asked, “Do ‘the bump,’ what’s that? It sounds like a dance step.” “Well kind of,” said Floyd, “that’s what Coach Moore calls it when you bump somebody over off their knees after you’ve got him locked up like you did.” “I didn’t know that,” said Robbie. “Yeah, that was pretty obvious,” kidded Floyd.

After Robbie’s loss, J.D. and Matt both won. Later at 189 Charles locked up a really tight ‘half nelson’ and got a pin. Danny’s opponent at heavyweight only weighed about 225, most of that baby fat, and Danny ‘bear-hugged’ him to his back for a quick pin in less than a minute. When all was finished the Pirates had their first win of the season, 33-18.

Chapter 10 – Do The Bump

Saturday found Robbie and Al shooting baskets out in the driveway again. Al had challenged Robbie to the "One-on-One World's Championship" and Robbie was up 4-3 when Jake Armstrong and his cronies wandered by. Jake was wearing a jacket but a cast was visible sticking out the end of the right sleeve. Jake called out, "Hey Robbie, how'd you guys do last night? You beat anybody yet?" Robbie replied, "The team won but I lost my match. It seems like the only guy I can beat is Jamie Byrd in wrestle-offs."

"I figured that much," said Jake. "If you get on the mat with that darkie Floyd Bennett, kick his butt for me. Him and his Black Power crap!" "I told you, Jake, Floyd's a good guy," said Robbie, "You just don't know him." "That's bull crap," said Jake, "He got lucky last time but next time I might shove this cast right up his nose and see how he likes that!" Jake's friends laughed as they envisioned Floyd's smashed face. Robbie held his ground this time and replied, "Look Jake, I told you not to mess with Floyd and look what happened to you. You'd best leave him alone." Jake then said, "Be careful about picking sides, Renfro, or you'll get your butt kicked too." With that they continued down the street with Jake fishing his pack of cigarettes out of a pocket with his good hand.

Just before practice Monday, Robbie told Matt about his run-in in the driveway and they both warned Floyd to be watching out for him. The 189-pounder Charles Longstrom had just walked in, smacked the "Go For It" sign for good luck and was lacing up his wrestling shoes. Overhearing the conversation he said, "Hey 'Door Matt,' point this guy out to me sometime."

Practice got started and after warm-up Coach Destin pulled out the clipboard and began going over mistakes from the Stark H. S. match to correct. When he got to Robbie's match at 130 he said that this would be a good time for the team to add the 'bump' option to our 'cross-face cradle.' "Not knowing how to 'do the bump' probably cost Robbie a win Friday night," said Coach Destin.

Coach Destin then grabbed Martin Haislip as his "dummy" to demonstrate and showed the usual steps of the 'cradle.' When Coach had stepped out in front and driven the head to the knee and then locked the cradle he stopped in that position. He then explained that frequently the wrestler could just "rock the cradle" here and roll the bottom man to his back. Sometimes, though, as with Robbie's opponent the bottom man is braced on hands and knees and just won't be "rocked." "In this case," said Destin, "it's time to 'do the bump.' From this position I can swing behind my opponent and switch sides so I can lean against his hips. Notice how I can use my feet in this position to push the bottom man over off his knees. That's the 'bump.' From here, the bottom man is in a weaker position and we can roll him to his back."

"I've gotta try that," said Robbie to Matt. Actually everyone did, as the coaches drilled the team on the new option, talking them through each step. Later in practice Robbie held his own in "live" three-somes and match wrestling. He was developing some confidence. With all the drilling he was starting to react faster, to "see things coming." In earlier practice matches he had been frustrated frequently by realizing all too late that an opening had occurred or a mistake had been made. At the end of practice Coach Destin reminded the team that their first home match would be Wednesday night with J.W. Welborn H. S.

The next morning before school Floyd opened his locker and began exploring the mass of books and papers. Almost immediately his face was shoved sideways into his poster of Malcolm X and he felt the hardness of Jake's cast on the back of his neck. Bully that he was, Jake enjoyed using his 50+ pound weight advantage. "I told you to get rid of that Black Power crap, didn't I," hissed Jake, "but you just wouldn't listen would ya?"

Jake suddenly released his grip on Floyd who was expecting a heavy fist any moment. It didn't come. When Floyd turned around he saw that the team's heavyweight Danny Bosworth had grabbed Jake and was shoving him into the small alcove leading into the adjacent classroom. Danny quickly had Jake pinned up against the closed door while teammates Charles Longstrom and James Woodson were staring down Jake's cronies. Jake's buddies looked like they wanted no part of the two varsity athletes. All 260 pounds of Bozworth was now nose to nose with Jake in the alcove. Only Danny could see just how wide open Jake's eyes had become. Jake tried to talk a good show saying, "Back off, I don't have no fight with you," but it came out in a high-pitched voice. Even Jake's buddies could sense the fear in it.

Still nose to nose with Jake, Danny growled, "It'll be a short fight with a lot of pain. Your pain. You're going to quit messing with Floyd or we're going to start messing with you, big time. You got that?" Adding to Jake's fear was his dismay at these three big white jocks defending Floyd. It just wasn't something Jake could comprehend. "Yeah, yeah, I got that," stammered Jake.

"One more thing," said Danny. "The way I see it, all you got is these two Bozos who won't even step in to help you out, and Floyd's got the whole team on his side. Remember that." With that, Danny released Jake who stumbled back into the hall with his two buddies, each of which quickly disappeared down the hall.

"Man, I thought I was a goner," said Floyd. "Thanks for bailing me out." "No problem little man," said Danny. "We stick together." "I don't think you're going to have any more problems with old "Jake-the-snake,'" added Charles, "His kind doesn't like to pick a fight he can't win. Hey, we'll see you at practice."

Chapter 11 – Home Opener

In the locker room after school the "buzz" was about Floyd's close call with "Jake-the-snake," as Charles had nicknamed Armstrong. Matt, as it turned out, had "eyeballed" Jake for Charles that morning and the team's three upper weights had taken over from there. As Robbie and Matt entered the wrestling room they noticed their pesky 103-pounder Justin sneaking up behind Danny who was reading the stat sheet on the bulletin board.

Justin then pounced on the big heavyweight, locking a 'scissors' hold around his waist with his legs while also catching a 'headlock.' "Christ," said Danny, "the flea's back. Let go or I'll fall down backwards and crush you!" "You wouldn't dare," said Justin, "you need me at 103 tomorrow night." Instead, Danny dropped down to both knees and began the process of peeling the pesky Justin off. Justin was strong for his size and a good wrestler so he managed to stall the inevitable for about a minute. Danny finally caught Justin by an arm and a foot, spun him around and threw him about twelve feet across the mat. Several wrestlers chuckled at the free entertainment. Justin bounced off the mat and darted out the door.

It was another "drill practice" for the Pirates with the home opener the next day. The only real wrestling they did was called "situation wrestling" in which Coach Destin would direct the team members into certain situations such as halfway through a 'double-leg' takedown or halfway through a 'switch' for a reversal and then blow the whistle. At the whistle one wrestler would attempt to complete the move while his partner tried just as hard to counter the move.

At the end of practice Coach Destin reminded the team that J.W. Welborn H.S. had won its conference championship last year though they had lost several seniors from that team. It still looked to be a tough dual meet. Coach pointed out that they had won a close one over them last season and if not for Mo Carmon, one of last year's seniors, we probably would have lost it.

Destin explained that Mo had failed his physical last year due to high blood pressure. He had gained a lot of weight during the off-season and reported back pretty chunky. The extra pounds had elevated his blood pressure somewhat and while the doctor would allow Mo to run and exercise, he wouldn't clear him to actually wrestle. Mo stuck with the team anyway and went to work trying to diet and run off the extra pounds. Getting his weight back down helped control his blood pressure as well, and he got the doctor's okay the week before last year's match with J.W. Welborn H.S. "His win at 215 last year helped us win the meet by three points," said Coach. "It'll probably be that close again tomorrow night but without Mo back we'll have to depend on others for that help." Robbie thought to himself, "I hope it doesn't come down to my match."

The next day after school Robbie headed to the locker room to check his weight. No overweight was allowed for matches, not even a quarter pound. Others came in checking weight and almost everyone was on the weight or a little under. James Woodson the 215-pounder ate all he wanted but still only weighed 205. The 215-pound weight class being for those weighing 215 or less. A couple guys were hanging around playing cards while a couple others were about a half pound over and were putting on some sweats to run it off. Robbie and Matt caught a ride with Charles down to the Quick-Pick to get a snack. Weigh-in was scheduled for 5:00 with the JV wrestling at 6:00 and the varsity following at about 7:30. A team meeting was set for 4:30.

At 4:30 sharp Coach Destin started the team meeting and explained that the main order of business was to get the gym set up for the meet. He wanted to get this done in the half hour before weigh-in but if necessary some might have to be finished later. J.D. and Artel tried to slip in the door late for the meeting and Coach quickly assigned them some extra push-ups. Destin then divided the team into four groups and assigned each group to a different senior. He had given each of the four seniors a 3x5 card with the names of his crew and the jobs they needed to get done. This was "old hat" for the returning wrestlers.

Matt and Robbie were assigned to Charles' group which had to move the competition mat into the gym. Each of the three sections of mat was 38 feet long, about 13 feet wide and weighed hundreds of pounds. Charles sent Matt and Robbie to the adjacent storage room for tubes to roll the mat up on. They looked like giant versions of the cardboard tubes aluminum foil is rolled up on. The main difference being that they were thirteen feet long and about a foot thick! They laid a tube down at one end of the mat and eight of the boys began rolling the mat up on it. The roll of mat got bigger as the boys rolled it across the mat. Rolling the mat up was new to Robbie and consequently he felt a little awkward. About half way across the mat his hand slipped and he fell over the roll of mat to the amusement of his teammates. "Roll him up in it," joked Charles.

Once they got the first section of mat rolled up, Charles sent for the set of mat rollers that were also in the storage room. Being pretty husky, Charles picked up one end of the rolled-up mat by himself while Matt slid a roller under it. They did the same at the other end and now the group could fairly easily roll the mat down the hall to the gym. Charles ordered his crew to "take it easy" and not steer the mat like Nascar drivers. Halfway to the gym Justin, who was in their group, jumped up on the mat and began riding it like a cowboy. Charles gave him a shove saying, "Hey, pull your own weight flea!"

As they pushed the mat into the gym Robbie could see that Danny's group had already pulled out half the bleachers and Martin's group was setting up chairs for the team "bench." Charles' group rolled the mat off the rollers and left it for one of the other groups to set up. Then it was back to the room for another section. The J.W. Welborn H.S. team showed up about that time and Coach Destin got them a locker room. Several of them wanted to check their weights on the Canady H.S. scale and others sat in the bleachers to talk and watch the gym set-up.

After the JV meet, J.W. Welborn's varsity took to the mat for warm-up. The Canady H.S. team had a final meeting in the locker room with Coach Destin reminding them, "Keep your head up at all times out there and be aggressive. Take the first shot." The team lined up in the gym lobby by weight classes and at the conclusion of the Welborn H.S. warm-up began rhythmically clapping hands while jogging into the gym and around the mat. There was a good crowd for the meet. While stretching out, Robbie peeked up into the stands and saw his parents sitting about 2/3 of the way up. This was the first wrestling meet either had ever attended. They were aware that this wouldn't be that "fake pro stuff" but weren't exactly sure what to expect. Both looked nervous and his mother seemed to be biting her lip. "Funny," thought Robbie, "I'm the one who ought to be nervous."

The two teams split the first four matches before Robbie's match making the team score 6-6. If anything, this added a little more pressure for Robbie. He had a great desire to win but his confidence was affected by losses in both the scrimmage and the first dual meet. Robbie looked his opponent right in the eye as they shook hands to start the match. "He doesn't look real confident either," thought Robbie.

His opponent's confidence was boosted, however, when Robbie failed to stop his 'single-leg' takedown and found himself losing 2-0. Robbie had practiced countering 'single-legs' since the team started practice but his opponent had caught Robbie leaning in and swept low to the outside and picked up his leg at the ankle and then neatly tripped him to the mat. Robbie struggled but found himself mostly tied up by his opponent. A minute into the match Robbie attempted a 'switch' for a potential reversal.

He failed to get behind for a two point reversal but did manage to escape from his opponent. "One, escape," declared the ref. Back on his feet, Robbie reached in to tie up his opponent's head and he again neatly shot under Robbie's outstretched arm and was back in on another 'single!' Again Robbie felt his leg lifted and soon was tripped hard to the mat. The first period ended with Robbie down 4-1.

Robbie started down in the second period and immediately stood up on the whistle only to be tripped back down to his stomach. With no quit in him he struggled back to his knees and tried the switch again, his only successful move thus far in the match. His opponent saw it coming this time and drove Robbie down hard to his shoulder. Instinctively Robbie used that motion to continue turning to his left and tried his 'turn-in roll.' This caught the J.W. Welborn H.S. wrestler off-guard and over he went. "Two, reversal," declared the ref.

Robbie was unable to hold him on his back but had tightened the score to 4-3. Robbie rode his opponent hard but he managed an escape and the second period ended with Robbie losing 5-3.

Starting on top in the third period Robbie knew he needed to turn his opponent to his back to earn a win and he worked hard to do that. With a minute left and still on top Robbie was still down 5-3 when they went out-of-bounds. As they returned to the center Coach Moore yelled out, "Step out and drive that head!" Resolved to do that Robbie tried his 'cross-face cradle' again on the whistle, stepped his left foot out in front for leverage, and drove his opponent's head to his knee. Locking the cradle but unable to rock his opponent to his back, Robbie heard Coach Moore yelling again, "Bump him Robbie! Do the bump!"

Robbie did just that and rolled his man to his back. As the referee began counting the seconds for a near fall, Robbie's opponent began pulling and twisting at Robbie's grip. Breaking the grip, the Welborn H.S. wrestler bridged over to his stomach as the ref called out, "Two, near fall." Robbie's parent's glanced up nervously at the scoreboard which now read 5-5. Robbie quickly found that there was no quit in his opponent either, as he worked up to his knees and worked to control Robbie's hands. Robbie couldn't hold him down and he successfully stood up, peeled the hands, and escaped. "One, escape," called the ref. Many anxious fans quickly glanced at the scoreboard as it changed to 6-5 visitors.

"Short time," yelled Coach Destin, "Shoot!" There were, in fact, only twenty seconds remaining as Robbie stepped into his opponent. Do-or-die, Robbie used both hands to pop his opponent on the head and shoulder and drove immediately into a 'double-leg' takedown. The set-up caused the

Welborn H.S. wrestler to pop his head back up momentarily as Robbie shot in. The follow-through worked just like in practice and Robbie completed the takedown as the home crowd cheered. After just a few seconds of riding the buzzer sounded. Briefly confused over the score, Robbie checked the scoreboard which read Canady 7, Visitors 6. Robbie couldn't help but smile broadly as his hand was raised. He was unaware of his tiredness and thought he had never felt better in his life! As he returned to the team bench, his teammates greeted him at the mat's edge. Floyd gave him a bear hug as Coach Destin patted him on the back saying, "Congratulations on your first varsity win."

J. D. and Matt won the next two weights but the dual meet score stayed close the rest of the night. Another win by Danny at heavyweight and the Canady Pirates finished on top 43-31 for the team's second straight win. After the meet ended,

Robbie met his parents on the gym floor. J.W. Welborn's team had headed for their locker room and many parents and fans were milling around. Robbie's mom gave him a hug while his dad patted him on the back and said, "Congratulations son. I couldn't follow all the action but I sure liked the final score! We sat with Kevin Hopkins' folks; I know him from work. He says you've been coming right along." "Thanks dad," said Robbie. About that time Charles Longstrom yelled, "Hey Renfro. Let's get this mat moved so we can go home." Robbie smiled and went back to work with his crew.

During the drive home Robbie's dad asked, "Who was that black boy who hugged you after the match? You worked with him during warm-up too." "That's Floyd Bennett, dad, the fellow I told you Jake Armstrong was picking on." "You wouldn't know this son," said his dad, "but I went to school with Jake's father and I'll tell you that the acorn doesn't fall too far from the tree. Jake's dad was in and out of trouble all the time and ended up dropping out of school. I wasn't much of a student myself, but I did stay out of trouble. In fact, I hear his dad's a pretty hard worker but still has trouble holding a job because he just can't get along with people." Jake's mom added, "It looks like Jake's headed down that same path if he doesn't get himself straightened out."

His dad then said, "I didn't realize there were that many black boys on the wrestling team." Robbie answered, "We've got a good team spirit, dad. Everybody helps each other out. In fact it was a couple of white guys who bailed Floyd out when Jake had him cornered. Coach Destin tells us that in wrestling it doesn't really matter what color you are or what neighborhood you're from but whether you can get the job done." "I can see that," his father acknowledged and drove silently the rest of the way home.

Chapter 12 – On The Road Again

The bell rang for first period the next morning and Robbie was sorting through his notebook for his English homework while morning announcements were being made over the intercom. Robbie paused as the team score for the wrestling meet was announced followed by the names of the winning wrestlers. When the name "Robbie Renfro" was announced Mr. Long smiled in his direction and said loudly, "Congratulations Robbie. Keep up the good work." Robbie got along well with his fellow students and several made compliments or kidded him. Bill, in the seat behind him, patted him on the back and kidded, "Way to go. It's about time you got something right." It was nice to get some positive attention in school and he received congratulations from several other friends during the school day.

Robbie ate lunch with Matt and Floyd and they discussed the previous night's meet in good spirits. Both said they felt Robbie was getting a "feel" for the mat action. "Yeah, I think I'm getting into the flow of things some now," said Robbie, "I feel like I'm reacting when things happen now instead of a little late." "Right, like when your face hits the mat," kidded Floyd. "Coach says the best wrestlers don't just react as things happen," said Matt, "they anticipate their opponent's moves <u>before</u> they happen." "Yeah," said Floyd, "That sounds like trying to wrestle Jeff Fencik when he's in town." "Who's that," asked Robbie. "Jeff was All-State here a couple years ago and he's wrestling for State U. now," said Matt. "He's really smooth on the mat." "I'll say," added Floyd, "I can never score a point on him unless he just lets me go. He usually works out with us during the college breaks.

At practice that afternoon Coach Destin reminded the team that they would be traveling to Lesterburg H.S. Friday night to take on the

"Lions." It was a tough practice conditioning-wise since they did a lot of "live" wrestling. It was fun, though, since most everybody would rather wrestle than drill. Robbie squared off with Floyd for a six minute match toward the end of practice and noted a definite change. While Robbie outweighed Floyd by ten pounds and was the stronger of the two, Floyd was quicker and more experienced. "Experience beats strength" was one thing the coaching staff said a lot and that had always proved true thus far with Floyd beating Robbie every time pretty handily, always by at least a few points. In today's match, though, Floyd had to fight for a late escape to squeeze out a win by one point. "Good match" they both said at the final whistle and this seemed to Robbie further evidence that he was catching on.

They did a couple more "change-of-pace" games at the end of practice. Coach Destin called the first one the "bear fight" and had each pair of wrestlers stand back-to-back with their arms crossed in their ten-foot practice circle. On the whistle they were to turn around quickly and try to shove the other "bear" out of the circle which looked pretty hard with your arms still crossed. "Shove that bear out of your den," yelled Coach after blowing the whistle. Robbie was grouped with Matt and J.D. taking turns in a 3-some and lost a couple more than he won. It was fun though, and a good workout.

The next game they tried was called "Indian wrestling." "I don't know if they used these rules," remarked Coach Destin, "but the American Indians did wrestle before the settlers arrived and most of the settlers knew some wrestling from their home countries." "What about us black settlers," joked Martin. "You might think you're kidding, Martin," said the Coach, "but many of the African tribes have wrestling traditions that go back hundreds, even thousands of years." He then described the game rules which involved laying face up on the mat with each wrestler's feet facing opposite from his opponent. On command, the "Indians" each raised a leg toward the ceiling and on a 3-count tried to throw the other man using the leg. Robbie got thrown by Matt but managed to throw J.D.

During announcements at the end of practice Coach Destin reminded the team members to be keeping up with their homework assignments and suggested writing on a calendar at home any tests they had coming up. He also reviewed some of his earlier suggestions about what they ate.

"Particularly for those of you on a diet, if you are having to limit what you can eat, then at least make sure that what you do eat is good food. This is especially true after weigh-in when you should just have an easily digestible snack like a piece of fruit. Nobody wants to see what they ate, twice"

After practice, Robbie asked Matt how Lesterburg's team usually was. Matt indicated that their Pirates had whomped them pretty good last year, "But that was last year. Just be ready for a good match."

Coach Destin echoed that sentiment at Thursday's practice, firmly announcing "Never underestimate your opponent! It's often a fatal mistake." This came up after Coach overheard Martin and Terrance bragging about how many points the team would likely run up on Lesterburg the next night. They got one practice match in amongst the mostly drill-practice and Robbie slipped by their 125-pounder Chris Farner 6-4. Another confidence boost.

Upon arriving at Lesterburg H.S. the next evening, Coach Destin parked the activity bus in a lot off to the side of the gym. He told everyone to check and make sure they had all their stuff and then led the group to the side entrance. At the entrance he stopped and waited for the team to regroup since they'd gotten all strung out taking turns getting off the bus. At that point Coach noticed Charles Longstrom standing a few feet away. In Charles' right hand was his team bag but in his left he was balancing an entire banana cream pie. Charles was busy talking to Danny and was surprised when Coach Destin stepped over and took the pie.

"What the…" said Charles before he saw who had taken the pie. Destin's eyes were wide open and his jaw was tight as he stood there staring at Charles. He was obviously pretty ticked off. "What the heck are you doing with a cream pie before the match," asked the obviously irate head Coach. "We've been talking about nutrition and a pre-match snack that's easy to digest your whole career and then you pull this kind of stunt!" "Coach," stammered Charles, "I didn't have much time after school and they were on sale down at the Quick-Pick." Unfortunately for Charles, there happened to be a trash barrel right by the doorway and Coach Destin slammed the pie down into the barrel saying, "That's what I think of your pie!" Charles looked like he wasn't sure whether he ought to cry over the loss of his cream pie or pick up Coach Destin and throw him into the barrel with it! A tense moment ended with Coach declaring, "We came here to wrestle not pig-out. Let's go in and check weight."

The meet was probably less exciting than the pie incident with Canady H.S. winning as expected by a 45-15 final score. Robbie and Matt were among the winners. Perhaps a bit too cocky the day before, Terrance had lost by a couple points in maybe his weakest match to date. Martin had his troubles too, early on, but "woke up" in the third period and took control of the match.

"We're undefeated," shouted Danny as the team boarded the bus afterwards. His workout partner James countered with, "It's still early, but 3-0 feels pretty good." As they all found seats on the bus, Danny yelled over to their 189-pounder, "Hey Charles, how about a piece of that pie!" "Oh, shut up," replied Charles over the laughter of his teammates. "Yeah Charles," said James, "I'd like some of that pie too!" Even Charles was smiling now and he replied, "Okay, okay, you got me." It was dark on the bus and a few heads leaned against windows taking naps while others were talking about the match.

Down the road an obnoxious odor began to become apparent. "Oh God that stinks," said someone in the back of the bus. "Kevin, was that you, you dog," said James. "That wasn't me, I claim my farts," replied Kevin their 171-pounder. Bus windows began sliding down as athletes feigned choking to death. "You guys are something else," exclaimed Coach Moore.

Kevin had his head up near the open window and his friend James called out, "You'd better not stick your head out that window. With those big ears of yours they'll get flapping and tear your head clear off!" Kevin fired back, "At least ugly doesn't run in my family the way it does in yours." "That's just the point, Kevin," said James, "I'm the prettiest in my family and you're the ugliest in yours." Their teammates were enjoying the good-natured banter. Coach Destin smiled in the darkness and shook his head while continuing the drive back to school.

Chapter 13 – Looking Ahead

At practice Monday there weren't too many mistakes to go over after Friday's overwhelming win. "It's more fun to win," said Coach Destin, "but we learn more from a tough loss." "If that's true," whispered Robbie to Matt, "I'd rather keep winning and stop learning so much!" Destin did mention possible overconfidence problems affecting Martin and Terrance's matches. Martin spoke up saying, "That's straight, Coach. I pinned that guy last year and really didn't think he could hang in there so tough with me. I learned that lesson."

"I'll repeat what I told you on Thursday gentlemen," continued Destin, "my old high school coach used to say it all the time, too. 'Never underestimate your opponent.' You have to be mentally ready when you step on that mat. You can't call a time out. If you're not mentally ready when you first step out there it's often too late as

Terrance found out Friday night. Martin managed to pull one out in the third period, but not by much."

After the talk they broke up into three-somes and wrestled takedowns. Robbie ended up in a group with Chris and J.D., the varsity starters at 125, and 135. Robbie held his own, getting probably half of the takedowns. In the three-somes Robbie went a takedown with Chris and then one with J.D. and then sat one out while Chris and J.D. went at it. Out-of-bounds during the three-somes was either when they strayed into another group's circle or ran into the padded wall. At one point Robbie stopped wrestling when he and J.D. hit the wall but J.D. kept at it and shoved Robbie flat up against the wall and declared, "Wall-Fall!" "It's nothing," said Chris, "J.D.'s saying that he pinned you against the wall and that sure doesn't count." "Well, the wall's got mats on it, doesn't it," kidded

J.D., "I just pinned you on a mat." "Very funny," said Chris, "but it still doesn't count."

After taking a water break and then practicing some moves, they went three-somes again. This time it was "mat three-somes." Robbie ended up in a three-some with his friend Matt and Jamie the JV 130-pounder. Robbie was now scoring in most situations top or bottom against Jamie but not often against Matt. They were doing 30-second three-somes today, which is to say that the whistle to stop came after thirty seconds whether anyone had scored or not.

They did a push-up/sit-up ladder at the end of practice again. Being in better shape now they started at ten push-ups and sit-ups and worked all the way down to one. That was 55 of each, and at the end of a two hour practice at that, so arms and stomachs were getting pretty tired towards the end. Robbie was able to thrust his chest up and clap on the last push-up, something he hadn't been able to do in the early practices. The team then did their "log run" while slapping the mat in unison. Robbie thought to himself, "Trying out was a good move for me. I was too shy to give it a shot last year."

After a few other announcements Coach Destin dismissed the JV team. Only the varsity would be making the trip to Washington D.C. this Saturday, he explained. "Let me give you a few guidelines about the trip. I'll give you more details as we get closer to it." He went on to say that the quadrangular meet would be at Yorktown H.S. It wasn't actually in the city but outside town in the suburbs.

We would have to meet at school before dawn Saturday, drive several hours to the site of the meet, make weight, and wrestle the three other teams that afternoon. "This is going to be an exciting trip for all of you but on Saturday afternoon you will need to shake the "trip" out of your system and focus in on your wrestling. Your opponents will be entirely focused on whipping your butts." He also pointed out that our wrestlers would be spending the night in the homes of the Yorktown H.S. wrestlers.

"This is called a cultural exchange. Though I don't know how much 'culture' we'll be taking up there from Laurentville," he joked. "Still," he continued, "it's a great chance to meet some families from the D.C. area and for them to meet us. There may be a few differences but basically we'll see that they are good people and we can find good people in every town and every race. Just remember that these people want to whip your tail on the wrestling mat before they take you home!"

That last comment got a few chuckles. At that point Charles joked, "I don't know Coach, if I pin my guy his folks may not want to take me home, or worse yet they might not bring me back!" That got some laughs and Destin immediately deadpanned, "Right Charles, but there would be some advantages to that for the rest of us."

Practice and school continued normally the next couple days, with one exception. Midway through practice Thursday 160-pound starter Terrance Ellison twisted his ankle during drills and was in obvious pain. Coach Destin sent for the school's athletic trainer, Mr. Grimm, and helped Terrance over to the side of the room. Terrance wasn't putting any weight on the ankle and his face was locked in a grimace. "Aww man, I can't miss that D.C. trip! Crap," he said.

Drills continued as Mr. Grimm examined the ankle. "I don't think it's broken, but I'll get you an appointment with Dr. Schwarz tomorrow just in case," said Grimm. "In the meantime," he continued, "you need to have plenty of pie." "Pie? What are you talking about," asked Terrance. Mr. Grimm just smiled and said, "You know, pie, P-I-E. You need **p**ressure, **i**ce, and **e**levation. We'll get that started tonight in the training room. We'll elevate your ankle, and use an Ace bandage for pressure and to keep the ice in place." "Ok, funny man," said Terrance who was now smiling. "I'm sitting here in pain and you're cracking jokes on me!"

During announcements at the end of practice, Coach Destin mentioned to Tyrelle Barnes, Terrance's JV back-up, that he'd be making the trip Saturday unless Terrance made a remarkable recovery. There were a few sideways glances at that point since, though athletic, Tyrelle was at best high-strung and at worst a little flaky.

Coach then went over a few details about the trip including the fact that we would take a drive-around tour of the city Sunday morning before driving back and possibly a ride on the Metro, the city's subway system. That idea brought some chatter since most had never ridden on a subway. There sure wasn't one in Laurentville, just an old freight line. "And by the way," Coach continued, "I was talking to the Yorktown H.S. coach on the phone last night and he mentioned that Katie Couric of CBS News had gone to school there. I thought that was pretty interesting." In an attempt at humor, Charles spoke up and asked "Did she wrestle there, Coach?" Destin just shook his head and replied, "Not to my knowledge. But if she did she'd probably whip ***your*** butt!" Danny shoved Charles in the shoulder as the team enjoyed a laugh on Charles.

Chapter 14 – Quad Meet

The team had the school van for the D.C. trip instead of the usual activity bus. It was a 17-passenger van and with 14 wrestlers, two coaches, a manager, and gear it was going to be a tight fit. They would make better time on the highway, though. The wrestlers met before dawn inside the building to check weight and get organized. For a while it looked like they were shorthanded, then Justin's dad dropped off Justin and Gary and they had all 14 starters. They only needed one change of clothes and most had mashed everything into their team bags with their uniform and shoes. Several guys brought along small coolers with snacks.

Coach Destin reminded the wrestlers that it was going to be a long day. It would be tough wrestling three teams after driving all morning so they should relax in the van and not burn up a lot of energy being excited about the trip. With that they loaded up the van, squeezing in like oversized sardines and stuffing their gear under the seats. For the first couple hours there was no concern about being excited about the trip. Before dawn was well before everybody's usual Saturday morning wake-up time and almost everybody was out like a light by the time the van was leaving town on the four-lane.

By mid-morning several wrestlers were listening to music on their headphones. Some of the guys in the back were using a cooler in the aisle as a card table and were playing a game. By noon, however, everyone was more than alert anticipating the activities of the weekend This had been especially true after the van had moved inside the Capital Beltway onto I-66. People had been asking Coach how much farther it was to the school and he had kept saying, "About a half hour." He'd been saying the same thing for a couple of hours and the joke had worn pretty thin. About 12:15 the van pulled past a Yorktown H. S. sign into the gym parking lot and Gary Newby excitedly asked, “Is this it? Are we there?” “Tired of riding in the van, heavyweight Danny Bozworth chimed in with, “No Gary, we told you it’s another half hour.”

They had taken one break on the way up, but everyone was more than ready to get out of the van and “get their legs back.” Weigh-in was scheduled for 1:00 with matches at roughly 2:00, 4:00, and 6:00. They were assigned part of a locker room and checked weights on the home scale.

There were two mats in the gym which would allow all four teams to compete at the same time, two on each mat. In a round-robin format each team would wrestle the other three in the quadrangular meet. Coach Destin reminded his athletes to stay hydrated but not to eat or drink too much at any one time to avoid feeling sick during competition. They should save their big meal for tonight after the last match.

Their first meet was against the South Capitol "Chargers." The Chargers forfeited two weight classes giving the Pirates twelve free points. It probably didn't matter since Canady H.S. won the match 40-17. Spirits were high for the Pirates at that point with both the long trip and their first win under their belts. The team stretched out after the match and then Coach Destin explained that after the short break they would be wrestling Clarendon H.S. which contended for its Regional title about every year in the area. "It could be our toughest meet of the day so let's not sit on our laurels. Be ready for a tough match."

Coach Destin's prediction proved true as the "Wolves" of Clarendon gave Canady H.S. everything they wanted and maybe a little more. Robbie lost a close match and felt about as bad when his friend Matt lost his first match of the year fifteen minutes later. Canady H.S. won most of the middle weights except at 160 pounds where Terrance's substitute Tyrelle lost and almost got ejected. His opponent had countered his double-leg takedown attempt with a forceful, but probably legal cross-face. Tyrelle lost his cool and looked like he wanted to take a swing at the Clarendon wrestler but the referee got him calmed down and he was able to finish the match.

Going into the last two weight classes, Canady H.S. needed wins at both to win the meet. James lost his match at 215, though and Danny's close win at heavyweight wasn't enough as Arthur L. Canady's wrestling team took its first loss of the season 39-34. Coach Destin had the team stretch out after the meet as usual, to avoid muscle soreness and then sat them down.

Destin told the team, "We had a good run to get to 4-0 and we lost our first meet today for probably two reasons: we weren't quite up to our best performance, and Clarendon has got a good solid team. We don't like to lose, but competing against tough teams like them will make us a better team too. The great football coach Vince Lombardi once said 'Winning is habit, but unfortunately so is losing.' We've got one more meet this evening and with a good effort we'll get back into that winning habit." The seniors on the team followed that comment with statements like, "That's right guys" and "Let's get it done."

The outcome of the Yorktown H.S. meet was more to their liking. Robbie and Matt both won close matches. At 189, Charles was winning a fairly close match when he caught his opponent in a headlock and pinned him for six team points. Going into heavyweight the Pirates were winning by five points. Yorktown's only hope was a pin at the last weight but Danny snuffed out that hope with a 7-1 win. The "decision" gave the Pirates three team points and the final score was 38-30 Canady.

With the win, Canady H.S.'s record stood at 5-1 overall after going 2-1 in the quad. Yorktown had to be satisfied with a daily tally of 1-2. After the meet, there were a lot of people from the four teams as well as parents from the stands milling around the gym floor and socializing. Coach Destin was talking to the Yorktown H.S. coach and eventually rounded up his Pirates for a short meeting on the mat.

Since there were two mats, both his Pirates and the Yorktown "Patriots" would each move a mat back to their wrestling room. After getting a shower the boys would meet back in the gym to get matched up with families of the Yorktown H.S. wrestlers. The main order of business was to establish a time to meet back at the school van the next morning for their proposed tour and the drive back home.

Chapter 15 - D. C.

Sunday morning the team met back at the high school for their scheduled drive-around tour of the city and the trip back home. Several of the guys were already stowing gear under the seats of the van while a couple others were standing on the sidewalk talking to their host families. For Tyrelle Barnes, frequently thought of as high-strung, the trip seemed to be just the thing. He was smiling, relaxed, obviously having a great time. Soon, all the team members had arrived, said their good-byes, and packed like sardines back into the school van. Off to see the sights of the nation's capital.

The trip seemed mostly downhill towards the Potomac River. This wasn't noticed by many who were comparing notes over last night's stay with hosts, their video games, activities, etc. Several had gotten in some sightseeing with their host families after the last match. As the van approached Rosslyn on the Virginia side of the river, the big-city atmosphere was obvious, with many more high-rise buildings readily in sight than in all of Laurentville. Easily.

As a bridge came into view, Coach Destin indicated that we would be crossing Key Bridge, named for Francis Scott Key of National Anthem fame. There were islands in the river and Coach pointed to a large one and indicated that it was Teddy Roosevelt Island and that the president had been a talented wrestler. We had never known him to lie to us, but sometimes Coach would come up with certain "facts" that were hard to believe. His brain must have been a virtual attic of trivia.

Across the river, we took a right onto "M" Street. It seemed strange to name a whole street after a letter of the alphabet, but it was a big city and maybe they had run out of other names. Further down we circled around a big statue and took a right onto the famous Pennsylvania Avenue and most of us realized that the White House must be around close by. Granted, we didn't expect to step inside and see the president. Coach Destin had indicated that being hours from home we would see some of the major monuments from the van and then head for Laurentville.

In a few blocks we could see the White House and managed to cruise by a couple of its sides before finding our way back to a different section of Pennsylvania Avenue heading toward the Capitol Building. I think everyone in the van was glad that it was Coach Destin who was stuck with the driving. Shortly, we circumnavigated the Capitol Building and seemed to be heading back towards the other monuments and the river. I missed it but some of the guys said they saw the Jefferson Memorial off to the left of the van. Most of us were focusing on the more readily visible

Washington Monument looming through the front windshield.

Next up was the Lincoln Memorial and Coach surprised us by pulling up to the curb (parking in the area was seemingly nonexistent) and announcing that we should all unload to jog up the steps and say “hi” to Mr. Lincoln. He would circle around the monument and meet us back at the front. We were excited enough that jogging up the monument steps, unlike those by the gym and school cafeteria, seemed like a fun idea. The jog slowed down to a walk quickly, though, as we approached a D. C. policeman with his hands on his hips and wearing a stern look. Matt said “Let’s tell him Robbie is a terrorist and see if he uses his stun gun.” This brought a few laughs, everybody picks on the rookie.

We all said “Hi” to Honest Abe, but apparently he wasn’t in a mood for small talk so we soon left. Matt and Artel slid down the wide, stone banister adjacent to the steps while the rest of us pretended we didn't even know them. Soon we were back in the van and heading across Memorial Bridge, this time, with a view of Arlington Cemetery on the hill. We turned onto the George Washington Memorial Parkway before reaching the cemetery and headed back towards Rosslyn.

Back in Rosslyn, Coach Destin surprised us by parking the van on a side street. He then announced that since most of us had never ridden on a subway (or for many, any type of train) we would do just that. He also pointed out that since the Rosslyn Metro station is uphill from the river, that they had had to dig a monstrously deep hole in order to get down below the level of the river. As such, the escalator we would be riding down to the train level on was said to be the longest in all of North and South America. Considering that there was only one escalator in the entire town of Laurentville, that sounded fine to us.

Arriving at the upper level of the station each of us had to put money in a large vending machine in order to get a fare card for the train. That done, we approached the turnstiles, inserted our tickets into a slot which allowed us to push through the turnstile and pick our fare card back up on the other side. We then, as a group, rode down on that longest of escalators.

J.D. called out "Don't trip. You'll be a bloody mess by the time you hit the bottom!" Not to be outdone, Chris Farner replied "I'd just like to have my bowling ball here and see how many people I could knock down!" "Man this thing is long," said Matt to Robbie as they stepped on. "I'm going to time the trip," and he activated the stopwatch feature on his wristwatch. Up ahead we could see an elevator coming down. Apparently, access to the elevator must have been across the five-lane street from the Metro station to make up for the angle of the escalator. At the bottom, Matt smiled at Robbie and said, "Two and a half minutes on an escalator, what a ride!"

Down at the bottom we grouped up and headed for the "orange line" platform from which we took the first train. The doors closed with a whoosh and off we went under the river back to the city. Coach had told us that to save both time and money we weren't really going anywhere but on the train. Leaving a station would require us to pay to get back on and we didn't really have the time. The first stop was at Foggy Bottom but we stayed on and headed for Farragut West. None of us had a good concept of just where we were in the city, but when the conductor announced Foggy Bottom, Charles called out "Danny, this must be your stop because if anybody has a foggy bottom it has to be you!"

Laughs ensued, but all Danny could come back with was "You'll pay for that back in practice, Charles!"

At the Farragut West station we stepped off the train and, never leaving the station, changed levels to the platform for trains heading back to Rosslyn. Soon, we were back under the river and as we were heading back up the escalator all agreed it had been a fun trip. Back at the upper level, we then had to insert our fare cards into another machine which kept them but allowed us to press through the turnstiles and return to the outside of the station. We were all able to do this routinely except Tyrelle. For some reason the machine just wouldn't accept his fare card and he was getting pretty frustrated about it.

Seeing this, some of the guys were good-naturedly poking fun at Tyrelle yelling things from the sidewalk like "That machine doesn't like you Tyrelle!" or "You're never getting out of there

Tyrelle!" Coach Destin had successfully used his fare card to exit the station but seeing Tyrelle's predicament called out to him to go check with the man in a nearby glass booth. Tyrelle did this and the uniformed employee in the booth quickly told him to take his fare card to a machine he pointed at, insert the fare card in that machine, and the machine would indicate how much money he still owed. Apparently, Tyrelle had not inserted the correct amount of money initially. A couple of fellows were still razzing Tyrelle, as guys will, as he walked over to the machine. There, a clearly tight-jawed Tyrelle looked at his fare card and looked at the machine. The employee had talked a little too fast for Tyrelle's comprehension and Tyrelle looked again at the fare card and again back at the machine.

The guys were still kidding Tyrelle a bit when he surprised everybody by yelling to the group that he was tired of their crap and marched back to the top of the escalator and disappeared down into the station! It was as if he had been swallowed down a huge concrete throat. Even Coach Destin's eyes had gotten kind of big as he soaked in the situation. He first approached the employee in the booth and asked him to please all-call for Tyrelle Barnes to please return to the upper level. The employee did this, but with no result. Still seeming pretty calm, Coach Destin then handed the keys to the van to Coach Moore and instructed him to have the team wait in the van while he went down for Tyrelle.

Coach Destin then disappeared, like Tyrelle, down that long escalator. As Destin neared the bottom of the escalator he could see that a train was pulling into the station and Tyrelle was on the platform ready to board! Coach Destin ran toward the train in what appeared to be a scene similar to that in the movie "The French Connection." Coach saw that he could not reach the car Tyrelle had entered in time so he rushed to the closest car and managed to jump aboard just before the doors closed. Whoosh, the train left the station and headed back under the river to Washington D. C.

At the first station Coach Destin jumped out onto the platform and looked forward toward the car Tyrelle had entered. Tyrelle stayed on the train so Coach jumped back in his car. The same scene repeated itself at the next station, Coach Destin jumped out on to the platform and this time Tyrelle left his car also. Tyrelle, obviously still very upset, walked up the stairs to the next level, saw he couldn't get out of that station either and headed back down to the platform level again with his Coach following behind. Tyrelle then walked down to the far end of the platform toward the tunnel entrance. Coach Destin, sensing that Tyrelle had calmed down somewhat, then approached him and got him to sit with him on a nearby bench. Coach indicated to Tyrelle that he knew he was mad at some of the guys for getting under his skin and asked Tyrelle if he was mad at him. Tyrelle said he wasn't mad at the coach, who then explained that he had brought 14 wrestlers with him on the trip and he would be in a lot of trouble with the principal if he didn't bring 14 back. "Tyrelle, you don't want to get me in trouble, do you?" Staring down at his hands, Tyrelle indicated that he didn't and Destin reminded him that the guys may have gotten on his nerves but they were still basically his friends and how about heading back? Tyrelle agreed and soon they were heading back under the river on the subway.

There had been a lot of conjecture and talk in the van during their absence, but when Tyrelle and the Coach were spotted marching back up the hill toward the van absolute silence erupted. Team members were afraid to say anything for fear they would set Tyrelle off again and silence ruled as the van worked its way through city streets back to the interstate. Safely back on the interstate and approaching the Capital Beltway, Danny remarked "Tyrelle, I didn't think they were <u>ever</u> going to let you out of that subway station!" Laughter followed quickly and even Tyrelle smiled sheepishly. Soon, a card game had started and the guys in the back of the van were figuring out a song to sing.

Chapter 16 – Edison Eagles

There was a lot of napping in the van by the time it returned to Laurentville that evening. As they reached the outskirts of town many of the athletes without cars were pulling out cell phones to call home for a ride. Robbie had folded his jacket up into a pillow and had been resting his head against a van window. Seeing that they were pulling into town he borrowed a cell phone and called home and his dad agreed to pick him up.

Back at home he grabbed something to eat while filling in his parents on the trip. He ran through the details of the three matches and then launched into the story of how their drive-around tour had come to a shocking conclusion with Tyrelle running off on the subway. It was still amazing to think that he would have done that, but it was starting to seem a little amusing in retrospect.

Robbie's dad then asked, "Isn't Tyrelle the black kid that got bumped up from the JV for the trip?" Robbie said, "Right dad," expecting a short sermon next about blacks being untrustworthy or such, but was surprised. "You know, two months ago I probably would have been the first to say that what Tyrelle did was just because he's black and that's the way they are," his dad said, "but I won't say that. Tyrelle sure pulled a stupid one up in D.C., that's for sure, but I've been really impressed by how good the team chemistry has been, white and black. I can see that Floyd's becoming a good friend of yours and it's also true that a couple of the black wrestlers are among your best team leaders. I see everyone on the team bench pulling for each other and I'm impressed." Robbie had to pick his lower jaw back up off of the table in order to say, "That's right dad," which was all he could manage under the circumstances.

Monday morning Robbie noticed that Tyrelle was still in school. Coach Destin announced at practice that Tyrelle's behavior on the trip had been inexcusable and that he had suspended him from the team for a week. He would be allowed to return after that time and "work" his way back on.

The talk in the locker room was still all about the fun had on the D.C. trip but Coach Destin emphasized that the focus had to change to the task at hand, which was Friday's home match with the Edison Eagles. They had done well earlier in their scrimmage at Edison but this match would count. Robbie was hoping that Queen was still at his weight since, with some experience now, he felt like he had a real shot at him.

At practice, the wrestlers were glad to see that their usual 160-pound starter Terrance was recovering from his ankle injury. For the next couple days he was supposed to practice moves on it only and not chance further injury by actually wrestling. The trainer had furnished him a stationary bike to exercise on during "live" wrestling. Coach Destin hoped Terrance would be able to actually wrestle on it by Wednesday, but against teammates smaller than him. If that went well, then he could work out Thursday against athletes his own size and get back into the line-up Friday. Matt mentioned to Robbie, "I'll bet Coach wishes he would have had Terrance on that subway instead of Tyrelle!" "Yeah," said Robbie, "We could have used him in the quad, too."

Monday's practice was a hard one. They did some running in the halls and on the steps, a lot of drilling, and a hundred "up-downs." In "up-downs" the athletes run in place and then sprawl their legs back to fall onto their stomachs on command before leaping back to their feet to continue running. Coach Destin or Coach Moore frequently led the "up-downs" themselves by jogging in the center and dropping down to the mat. Upon seeing this, the wrestlers were to react immediately by sprawling their legs back, so it was a conditioning drill that also had a technique purpose, that of sprawling to prevent a takedown.

"Up-downs" were never any fun though, so to change the pace sometimes the coaches would have the athletes run a couple laps around the room run backwards, or call on the seniors to lead. The seniors would sometimes "fake" a sprawl to fool the unwary into sprawling too soon. This always got a few chuckles because those fooled still had to get back up and do the next "up-down" with the group.

They wrestled one practice match that day and Robbie took on his friend Matt who won, as usual. Robbie gave him a good workout but ended up on the short side 4-2. He had managed only two escapes for a point each while Robbie had completed both a takedown and a reversal for two points each. At the end of the match, Robbie complained to Matt that he could never seem to catch him in his ‘turn-in roll’ for a reversal even though he felt that he was doing it correctly.

Matt replied, “Look, I wrestle you every day so I can ‘feel’ it coming before you hit it. That’s probably why you can score with it against some of the other teams but not on me. Another thing, Coach says Jeff Fencik will be on college break starting next week and should make some of our practices. He’s a great ‘roll man’ so maybe you can pick up some pointers from Jeff.” That sounded good to Robbie, advice from someone actually wrestling for a college team.

By Thursday, bad luck seemed to be hitting the team two weeks in a row. It looked like the team would have Terrance back in the line-up at 160 pounds but now Gary Newby, the team’s 112-pounder was home sick. Word was that he had the flu and would be out until next week. That meant that Jerry Smith, the JV 112-pounder would have to fill in. Robbie never worked out with Jerry because of the size difference. Jerry seemed to be doing okay at the JV level, but the main thing that Robbie remembered about him was that on the first day of practice he had needed to go to the bathroom to be sick after running the hall laps and steps. Well, he looked like he'd gotten in better shape since then anyway.

At Friday night's weigh-in Robbie found out that he had the same opponent, Queen, who he'd lost to in the scrimmage with Edison and that suited him fine. Queen seemed confident. Upon stepping off the scale he smiled at Robbie and declared, "Good, I've got you again." The weigh-in had been very routine except at the 112-pound class when Jerry, the usual JV wrestler, had tripped on his way up to the scale. Apparently, he had been staring at his opponent instead of looking where he was going.

The meet itself got off to a good start for the Canady Pirates. At 103 pounds, Justin took his opponent down skillfully and then threw in a 'leg ride.' Justin had the poor fellow virtually tied up in knots before pinning him ten seconds before the end of the first period.

That brought an obviously nervous Jerry Smith up for his first varsity match. Sensing his nervousness, Coach Destin had been rubbing his shoulders and talking to him before patting him on the back and wishing him luck. As he jogged out, Jerry caught his foot on the edge of the mat and, like in the locker room, had to catch his balance. He didn't fall down but it had to be embarrassing though. Jerry's opponent really didn't look too tough and Gary Newby had easily beaten him in the scrimmage.

Jerry's nervousness caused him to have a poor stance and he was quickly taken down. He never seemed to get his bearings and while struggling to stay out of trouble he couldn't seem to get on offense and score. He managed to last until midway through the second period when, forgetting to turn away from his opponent's 'half-nelson,' he was rolled over and pinned. At that point Robbie got up off the bench to warm-up and overheard the coaches talking. Coach Moore was asking Destin, "Coach, what do you think was wrong with Jerry tonight?" Coach Destin replied, "That boy was so tight he could have taken a crap in a 'Texas Pete' bottle!"

Floyd pinned his opponent in the third period followed by Chris winning a close decision. And then it was Robbie's turn. Robbie remembered his 4-0 loss to Queen in the scrimmage and was determined to gain revenge. Queen appeared confident as he stepped on the mat. Perhaps too confident. He had actually smiled and winked at someone up in the stands on his way out to the center circle.

In their first match, Queen had shot a 'double-leg takedown' shortly after the ref's whistle started the match and Robbie nervously had forgotten the defense he had drilled all week. Not so, tonight. Queen again took a takedown shot shortly after the whistle started the match but Robbie routinely blocked both of Queen's shoulders with his hands. The action caused both to sprawl to the mat on their knees. Queen, obviously surprised to have his shot blocked so easily worked back to his feet but in a sloppy fashion that Robbie saw as an opening.

Robbie immediately popped Queen's head with his snap-and-go set-up and shot his own 'double-leg' takedown. Due to Queen's sloppy stance Robbie easily penetrated into his legs, and driving his head against Queen's hip drove him to the mat. The referee signaled, "Two, takedown." Simultaneously, Robbie's confidence grew as Queen's shrank. Robbie kept the pressure on and progressed to a solid 6-2 victory. "Revenge is sweet," thought Robbie as the referee raised his hand. Most of his teammates were just as successful and the team went on to a solid dual meet win.

Chapter 17 – Jeff Fencik

When Robbie entered the wrestling room for practice Monday he found Matt stretching out with a stranger (at least to Robbie) over in the corner. Robbie sat down next to Matt and got introduced, "Robbie, this is Jeff Fencik." They shook hands. Fencik had a grip like a vise though he was only about Matt's size. He had a confident, positive look about him. "Robbie tells me you've got the makings of a good roll but could use a few pointers. Let's work on it a little after practice today." Fencik had a way of firmly looking you right in the eye as he spoke. Initially, Robbie was a little slow to return the eye contact, focused as he was on the words "State College Wrestling" on Jeff's t-shirt.

"Matt tells me you might work out with us some during your break," Robbie said, "You must be really good to be wrestling at the college level." "Well, you have to make the transition to the college level," Fencik replied. "High school sports are tougher than middle school sports but kids make that adjustment. It's the same way when you move up to the college level. You have to train harder and improve your technique but people make the adjustment."

"Jeff, what do you think was the toughest adjustment you've had to make?" asked Matt. Fencik smiled and replied, "At the high school level the other guy is just trying to beat you, to win the match. At the college level it seems like the other guy is trying to beat you up! It's just more physical at that level since all of your opponents are basically grown men. Like I say, you adjust to it though, since by the time you get to college you're more physical yourself." Robbie soaked in every word. He had seen plenty of college sports on TV but had never really had such close contact with a successful college athlete before.

About that time Coach Destin told the seniors to get warm-up started and the team progressed through its usual stretches, jogging, and exercises. At the end of warm-up the Coach told the team to sit with a partner while he introduced a "special guest." Destin mentioned that the returning wrestlers were very familiar with Jeff Fencik, either as former teammates or having met him last year, his freshman year at State College, when he had worked out at A.L Canady during college breaks. For the rookies, especially, he wanted to point out that Jeff was a great example of the type of student-athlete they were all trying to become. First of all, he said, Jeff had been an excellent student and was well prepared to move on academically to the college level. Secondly, Jeff was a hard worker and skilled athlete who had made All-State for Canady H.S. his junior year. But thirdly, and maybe most importantly said Destin, Jeff had overcome the hardship of a serious knee injury his senior year.

Jeff, he said, couldn't even compete in the Regionals his senior year much less contend for All-State honors again. As such, Jeff was basically un-recruited coming out of high school but had a burning desire to find out if he could compete at the 'next level.' He first had to rehabilitate and strengthen his injured knee during the spring and started competing again in summer events. Fortunately, he was academically solid enough to be accepted to the college of his choice and informed the head coach there that he'd like to 'walk on' and try out for the wrestling team. As a freshman Jeff had gotten some matches in but had mostly served as a back-up to one of the team's upper classmen. Now, as a sophomore, Jeff had made the college team's starting line-up.

Robbie had a chance to go “three somes” with Matt and Jeff during practice and it was quite a workout. Robbie always had to go 100% just to stay with Matt, with limited success. But he had NO success against Jeff, scoring absolutely no points against him in their several short bouts in the three-somes. He didn’t feel too bad, though, since Matt hadn’t scored on him either. Jeff didn’t even seem to be working hard most of the time. He was so smooth. He just very mechanically worked his technique from set-ups and seemed to “feel” any shots coming from either Matt or Robbie. Robbie had gotten in on Jeff once with a tight ‘single-leg’ takedown attempt but Jeff had merely stepped it up a gear and fought him off.

When Coach Destin blew the final whistle, Jeff smiled and poked Matt in the shoulder declaring, “Tough luck. Looks like you’re still the ‘Matt-burn,’ at least for me.” Matt replied, “That’s okay. That was a heckuva workout. You've got to show me a couple of those set-ups after practice." They soon did. After practice Fencik spent several minutes showing Matt how to better 'set-up' his favorite takedown. Robbie soaked up this free advice and tried a couple himself.

After the takedown work Jeff remembered that Robbie wanted some help to score more consistently with his 'side roll' from the bottom position. Jeff told Robbie, "Use Matt as your partner and show me what you do." Robbie demonstrated a typical 'side roll' starting with a 'sit-out,' grabbing Matt's right wrist, turning in to his left shoulder, and then rolling Matt over to his back. Jeff watched intently and then said, "Okay, do it again." Robbie did as he was directed and then Jeff asked, "Do you know how to do an 'elevator?'" Robbie just stared back at him, confused, and Matt spoke up saying, “He doesn’t know that one yet, Jeff.”

Jeff then said, “From what you two say, Robbie is able to hit the ‘turn-in’ and roll but his more experienced opponents manage to slip back behind him at the last moment. Robbie, I think that if you can add the ‘elevator’ to what you’re already doing then you’ll score more consistently. Let’s face it, you won’t score on everybody, no move is perfect, but you will pick up some more reversals. Matt, take top and we’ll show Robbie what I’m talking about.”

Jeff took the bottom position and duplicated Robbie’s usual ‘sit-out,’ ‘turn-in,’ and ‘side roll’ mechanics. He stopped when he got to the point in which he was about to roll Matt over to his back. Jeff then said, “Robbie, from what Matt is saying you get to this position against the tougher guys and they manage to slip behind you as you try to roll them over. Is that about right?" Robbie agreed. "Ok," continued Jeff, "In order for Matt to slide behind me from this position he's got to get past my feet. Look at my left foot which I just hooked on his leg. Matt, can you go behind me now?" asked Jeff. Matt acknowledged that he couldn't because Jeff's left foot was blocking his leg.

"All right," said Jeff, "Now this all happens pretty fast in a match, but if you catch the top man's leg with your foot he can't slide behind you. Then, as you continue your roll motion you can 'elevate' your left leg which gets the top man off balance, and over he goes." Jeff demonstrated by kicking or 'elevating' his left foot against Matt's leg and rolling him right over onto his back. "Wow, that could work," said Robbie, "Let me try it." "Not yet," replied Jeff, "Watch it again first and then I'll hit it on you so you can feel it as well as see it." They did that and then Robbie gave it a try.

At Jeff's instruction he took it slow at first and gradually picked up speed as he became more comfortable with this new 'follow-through' for his 'side-roll.' After several repetitions Jeff declared, "I think you're getting a feel for it. What do you think?" "Thanks Jeff, this could pay off," said Robbie. "You're going to need to keep practicing that," said Matt, "but I think you've got it. Maybe you'll be ready to give it a shot by the Cloverdale Tournament this weekend."

The next day during practice Robbie put special emphasis on the 'elevator' follow-through to his 'side-roll.' It was fun to learn a new move, or at least improve on one he already knew. Neither Matt nor Robbie did very well against Jeff Fencik in live wrestling though they again got a great workout, and they both got to drill moves with him and pick up a lot of pointers. It was like working out with your own personal coach.

At the end of practice the team sat down, as usual, for announcements. Coach Destin pointed to the back wall of the wrestling room and said that having Jeff Fencik back in the room reminded him of the "Use Your Block" concept. The back wall of the wrestling room was a cinder block wall which, up to about head-height, was covered with alternating purple and gold mats for safety. He pointed to a line of 19 ½ cinder blocks running across the wall that had all been outlined in purple magic marker. Robbie had seen and ignored this line of blocks, not seeing any significance in them.

Coach Destin explained that there were 19 ½ cinder blocks in the line. The ½ block was the first one on the left, he said, and represented your first two years of life. The other 19 each represented four years of life for a total of 78 years, the average adult life span. The fourth full block from the left was painted purple and, he said, represented your four years of high school. That one block out of 19 ½ was a visual representation of the athlete's entire high school career. "So use your block," said Coach Destin. "Don't be one of those athletes that procrastinates, puts things off and then at the end of their high school career has a lot of regrets. Jeff Fencik, for example, 'used his block.' He hustled and worked hard here at the high school level and now he's being successful at the college level."

Robbie, Matt, and Jeff stuck around after practice again, got in a run and then drilled some moves. This time included some free coaching from Jeff. Jeff mentioned that he'd still be in town this weekend and looked forward to seeing them wrestle at the Cloverdale Tournament.

Chapter 18 – Cloverdale

Practice had just gotten underway Wednesday when Jeff Fencik arrived. He walked in wearing a State College Wrestling t-shirt again and some workout shorts. When Coach Destin saw him he stopped warm-up temporarily and picked up a purple and gold t-shirt he had stowed over by the wall. He held it up and said, "Jeff, we want to get you back into Canady colors so we got you a team shirt. You can wear it Saturday when you help coach." This year's shirt, at first glance, looked like a Hard Rock Café shirt. It was pretty cool. It had a similar round logo but instead of the usual wording, stated "Head Lock Café" on the circle and "Canady Wrestling" below. Smiling, Jeff took off his college shirt and put on the new one saying he'd get it washed and wear it again Saturday.

Robbie continued to practice his usual moves and counters as well as the new 'elevator' follow-through for his 'side roll.' He hadn't been able to actually score on anybody with it at practice yesterday. Because, he figured, his teammates had been practicing their defenses a lot longer than he had been practicing the 'elevator.'

Midway through practice they got the chance to get in a practice match. Matt bravely squared off against Jeff while Robbie took on Floyd. Robbie's recent bouts with Floyd had all been close. Robbie was a little bigger and stronger while Floyd's superior quickness and experience usually won out. In today's match Floyd got in on a great shot with a 'single-leg' takedown but Robbie was able to push Floyd's head down, get his weight on him, and counter the move. Late in the period Robbie hit a smooth 'double-leg' takedown when he caught Floyd leaning in off-balance and was able to follow through the takedown due to his greater strength. Floyd quickly got hand control and escaped but Robbie felt good about the successful takedown.

Robbie ‘rode’ Floyd for a while in the second period but Floyd’s quickness made him a tough one to hold down and he escaped to tie up the practice match 2-2. They went about even through much of the third period with Robbie starting down. Robbie finally managed a good ‘turn-in’ after his ‘sit-out’ and attempted to reverse Floyd with his roll. Floyd’s quickness in sliding around behind Robbie had always prevented him from rolling Floyd over for a reversal. This time, though, Robbie managed to catch his left foot on Floyd’s leg and ‘elevate’ him over before he could slip behind. A surprised Floyd Bennett quickly found himself fighting off his back. Floyd bridged over to his stomach but Robbie was confident that, in a real match, he would have scored both a reversal and near fall points.

The match ended and the two shook hands. Floyd patted his teammate on the back and said, “That was a great ‘roll’ Robbie, you really caught me with that 'elevator.' You picked that up from Fencik, didn't you?" Robbie agreed and mentioned that he and Matt and Jeff were getting in some extra work after practice. Floyd shook his head and chuckled, "My girlfriend gets mad if I don't call her every day right after practice but I may have to join you guys anyway." Floyd then did that, making it a foursome after practice, getting in a run, some drilling and a little wrestling. Each peppered Jeff with questions about technique or about being away at college and soaked in his answers.

Friday marked the last day of classes at Canady before the Christmas break. Most of the students' minds (if not the teachers) were already on the break. Mr. Long wasn't on vacation yet though, and Robbie's English class was assigned an essay to write in class. The essay was to cover something they planned to do over the break; it could be a family gathering, a planned trip, etc. Robbie started writing about the Cloverdale Tournament. Since he'd never actually competed in a tournament before, his knowledge was limited on the topic so he focused mostly on the team's preparations. He wrote a paragraph about Jeff Fencik's recent contributions to the team and his success at college. Neither of Robbie's parents had attended college but, for the first time, he realized that his interest in wrestling was starting to make him think about moving up to the college level himself.

At practice that afternoon Coach Destin drew an eight-man bracket up on the white-board and explained some details about Saturday's holiday tournament. There would be a total of eight teams competing in the event at Cloverdale High School over in the next county. Each varsity starter would compete in his own weight class. It was a double-elimination tournament meaning, that all losers still had a chance to wrestle-back for third place. There would be medals for the top three in each weight class as well as a team championship. It would be a tough event, Destin noted, but Canady H.S. should be one of the teams contending for the team title. "The team's success," he said, "will be dependent on the focus and preparation of each of you starters."

Pointing to the bracket he had drawn, Destin explained that the tournament's eight entrants at each weight would be "seeded." Seeding, he explained, was an effort to separate the top athletes at each weight. "If you just drew it out of a hat," he said, "you might have the two best wrestlers competing with each other in the first round and that's not really fair." He also explained that the term "seed" means basically that each entrant is "planted" at a spot on the left side of the bracket and you then see who "grows" all the way out to the finals. It sounded a little like "March Madness."

Early the next morning the Canady team bus pulled onto the Cloverdale H.S. campus and parked down near the gym. There were already several cars and three other team buses present. The team members, carrying gym bags and small coolers filed into the gym entrance, most wanting to find the official scale and check weight. Everyone had been on weight in the Canady H.S. locker room but school scales had been known to vary some.

As they walked through the gym they could see two of the other teams hunkered down in the bleachers. Critical eyes from each team tried to guess who might be their opponents and judge how tough they looked. Three mats were down on the gym floor laying side by side, completely covering the basketball court. A couple wrestlers, bundled up, were jogging around the gym trying to lose that last ¼ pound. Another team was still in the locker room checking weight.

After weigh-in, the Canady Pirates got dressed and headed back to the gym to await the start of the first round, still over an hour away. Some of the guys snacked in the bleachers while a few were laid out on the mat playing cards to stay relaxed. Robbie, Matt, Floyd, and Jeff sat together on the mat. Jeff explained that they would be sitting up on those hard bleachers all day and, besides, wrestlers liked to hang out on the mats.

Jeff recounted how he had medaled for the first time in a college tournament earlier in the season. He had, he said, lost in the first round to the returning champion but came back to win several consolation matches, including two overtimes, to claim third place. "It wasn't a championship," said Jeff, "but the way I had to fight back I'm real proud of that bronze medal." Robbie had never won a medal, at anything, but he could well imagine.

Coach Moore had been hanging out with the wrestlers in the gym while Coach Destin attended the "seeding meeting." When Destin returned he was carrying a copy of the tournament bracket sheets. He then got the team together on the corner of one of the mats and went over each wrestler's seed and first round opponent.

Justin was seeded first at 103 pounds and had a first round "bye" because one of the teams didn't have a 103-pounder. He automatically advanced to the semi-finals. Several Canady H.S. wrestlers were among the top seeds. Matt was seeded first at 140 while Floyd was seeded second at 119. Robbie was seeded fourth at 130 pounds. His record was good, but his limited experience probably cost him a higher seed. Coach Destin then reminded the team that seeding helps spread out the talent, but who wins is decided on the mat, not at the seeding meeting. "You've got to go hard out there today against every opponent. Don't get hung up about the seeding," he said. "Remember, take 'em one at a time!"

At the end of the quarter-final round the team scores were close but Canady had advanced ten of their fourteen wrestlers into the semi-finals and was in first place. Robbie had not only won his opening match but had scored the first pin of his career!

His 'snap-and-go' set-up had worked smoothly and he had scored almost immediately with his 'double-leg' takedown. He had then confidently run out in front of his opponent trying to lock up a 'cross-face cradle' and had rushed it, gotten sloppy, and his opponent had escaped. Robbie went right back to his 'double-leg' takedown again and, as he drove his opponent down, noticed that he had hesitated on his side so Robbie automatically had thrown in a 'half nelson' and turned him to his back. After a brief struggle,

Robbie had secured the first period pin. A big smile was still on Robbie's face as Coach Destin and Matt met him at mat-side. "I'm starting to catch on," he said to Matt." "We must have practiced going from the 'double' to the 'half' a hundred times but that's the first time I've seen it quick enough to score with it." "Great," said Matt, "You're starting to react out there instead of having to think about everything."

Next up for Robbie would be his semi-final opponent, Johnny Pinner. Robbie hoped his opponent would not live up to his last name, "Pinner." He had to admit that it was a good name for a wrestler, though. Pinner was the returning champion and both Matt and Jeff had seen him wrestle in past years. He was known to have a good 'fireman's carry' takedown, a move Robbie wasn't particularly good at countering. In a 'firemen's carry' the offensive man grabs his opponent's upper arm and pulls down while dropping down to his knees and catching the inside of his opponent's leg. Halfway through, it looks kind of like how a fireman picks up a rescue victim. Pulling the arm down gets the defensive man off-balance and he frequently finds himself doing a forward roll onto his back. Robbie knew this all too well having been taken down with the move before.

In the semi-final bout it was senior versus sophomore and Robbie struggled to hold his own. Pinner got Robbie to step into him and launched him over with the 'fireman's carry.' He also scored a near fall before Robbie struggled to his stomach. Only 30 seconds into the match Robbie was down 4-0. That's how the match went. Pinner seemed to have an answer to everything Robbie threw at him. Robbie managed to go the distance but lost 12-3, gaining the three points on "give-away" escapes when Pinner chose to move back to his feet and go takedowns.

Robbie was disheartened by the loss and Coach Destin put his arm around his shoulder and, walking him to the bleachers, explained that he was still alive for third place. Two more wins and he could earn the bronze medal. The wins would also help the A.L. Canady team score. The team won seven of its ten semi-final matches, thus advancing seven wrestlers, including Floyd and Matt to the tournament finals. The rest of the team was still "alive" in the consolations.

In the consolation rounds, three of their teammates lost matches and were eliminated from the tournament. Robbie won his consolation semi-final match 6-3 to advance to the third place matches. Third place brought both a medal and extra team points to the winners. Before the consolation finals started Coach Destin sat the team down again and explained that placing eleven of the team's fourteen starters in the top four in their weight classes showed good team balance. The team race was still tight, however, and these final matches would determine which team took home the championship trophy. “We can beat these guys,” added Coach Moore.

A break occurred during which the host Cloverdale team rolled up one of the three mats and took it back to the wrestling room. The 14 consolation finals matches, one per weight, would be wrestled on the two remaining mats. Being at 130 pounds, the fifth weight class, Robbie would wrestle the third match on Mat 1. At the conclusion of the consolation finals another mat would then be rolled up and the 14 championship finals matches contested on the remaining mat in the center of the gym.

Robbie was scheduled to wrestle the number three seeded wrestler who had a record similar to his, but had more experience. Robbie had learned the hard way that the only way to beat these more experienced athletes was to out-hustle them. Robbie took the first shot of the match but was unsuccessful. They traded shots, both hustling, and then midway through the first period his opponent managed to slip behind him for a takedown and a two point lead. Robbie fought back by attempting a 'switch' and then a 'roll' without scoring. Late in the period they got into a flurry and Robbie managed to grab one of his opponent's legs. Though he was wrestling from the bottom position, he was able to twist around so that he was nearly facing his opponent and grasped his opponent's other leg as well and then, with a lift, reversed him with a move much like a 'double-leg' takedown. The first period ended 2-2.

In the second period Robbie rode his opponent effectively for the first minute and nearly locked him up in his 'cross-face cradle' at one point.

He could hear Coach Moore yelling from the corner, "Lock it up, Robbie!" His opponent managed to square off and avoid danger, eventually getting wrist control and hitting a 'stand-up.' His opponent was then able to pop his hips out and turn for an escape and a resulting 3-2 lead.

Down 3-2 going into the third period, Robbie started in the down position knowing he needed to score a reversal to win the match or possibly a one-point escape to take the match into overtime. His opponent, conversely, knew that he would win the match if he could just ride Robbie out the length of the period. Experience seemed to come into play as Robbie's opponent skillfully stayed behind him and smoothly countered every attempt. Robbie kept hustling, but not scoring. At the one minute mark Coach Destin called out, "He's stalling ref, make him wrestle," but to no avail. "Keep pushing him, Robbie, he's starting to 'gas,'" yelled Matt.

Robbie's extra workouts with Matt, and more recently Jeff, allowed him to keep the pressure on for the full 6-minute match. With thirty seconds left Robbie faked a 'switch' to his right and then turned left looking for his 'roll.' His opponent started, a little too late, to slide behind and Robbie's left foot caught his leg and he was able to use the 'elevator' to follow through the 'side roll' and dump his weary opponent unceremoniously onto his back. "Two, reversal," called out the referee as he started to count for near fall points. Too exhausted to fight off his back, his opponent retained enough pride to fight the pin and the match ended in the near fall position. The 3-point near fall finalized the score at 7-2 for Robbie.

Robbie's teammates congratulated him on his victory and Coach Destin added, "I still like that hustle, Robbie. Keep it up." Matt and Jeff were particularly enthusiastic and Robbie was careful to thank Jeff for his help with the 'elevator.' Jeff replied that the match may have come down to that one technique, but really his six minutes of hustle had won the match. "He just couldn't stay with you that last minute."

Awards were presented in his weight class after the 130-pound finals. At the awards table Robbie's bronze medal was hung around his neck by its long red, white, and blue ribbon. Proud of it, he thought to himself that it wasn't the gold medal but it was golden to him tonight. Justin, Matt, Terrance, Charles, and Danny each won championships to propel the Pirates to the team championship.

After the event, as the mats were being rolled up and the bleachers pushed in Coach Destin sat the team down for the day's final meeting. He congratulated the team for the championship and emphasized that it was indeed a team victory since every match won had added team points. Charles' mom, Mrs. Longstrom, got the coach to line up the team for a group photo, coaches, trophy and all. It was easy to get the group to smile.

Robbie's parents had attended the tournament. His dad had given him a hearty handshake and a pat on the back. His mom had given him a hug and said how proud she was of him. Robbie said, "Mom, I want you to wear this tonight," and placed his medal around her neck. "I'll be proud to wear it," she said, "at least until we get home." When they got to the car she mentioned that they had a little something for him, too. "We asked Coach Destin what would be a good Christmas gift for a wrestler and he suggested a pull-up bar. We thought you might as well get it early so you can use it. Your father installed it in your bedroom doorway this morning."

The wrestling room had several pull-up bars on the walls and doing pull-ups for grip and pulling strength was a regular part of their workouts. Robbie decided to start doing extra sets every day, when he got up in the morning and just before he went to bed. He felt that he was already pretty strong and could do nine or ten at a time. But with greater grip strength would come better control.

Chapter 19 – The Capital City Classic

“Hey Robbie, take a look at this,” called out his dad Sunday morning. He was reading the paper in the living room. He always read the Sports section first saying, “I like to start out with something I enjoy, then get to the ‘bad news’ later.” Robbie had gotten up later than his father and was just getting some breakfast. “What is it,” he called out from the kitchen. “You got your picture in the paper,” his dad yelled back.

That statement quickly brought both Robbie and his mom into the living room to take a look. Right there on the front page of the Sports section was the group photo of the team that Mrs. Longstrom had taken the night before. She must have e-mailed it to the paper. The photo appeared under the headline “A.L. Canady Champions.” An article including the tournament results followed under the photo. Robbie was getting used to seeing his name in the paper in the team results, and was developing a collection of clippings, but this was the first time he had gotten his picture in the paper for anything.

"Wow, that's great," exclaimed Robbie. "Well, how about that," added his mother. "We'll have to stop on the way to church and pick up a few more copies. I know your grandmother would love to have one and some others, too." "Yeah, that's my boy," said his father, "right there in the front row next to Matt. Is that Charles and Danny holding the trophy in the back row?" "That's right," answered Robbie. Several of the wrestlers were wearing medals around their necks.

In his excitement, Robbie called up Matt wanting to talk about the team championship and especially the photo. Having been an active athlete for several years, the photo wasn't quite as big a deal for Matt, but it was clearly a "keeper." Wednesday would be Christmas Day and the team was taking a break from practice until Friday. Matt mentioned that he was planning to get in a run every day to stay in shape, despite the cold weather. Robbie agreed that he would too, and added that his folks had gotten him a pull-up bar yesterday which he was already using. “Have you gotten any stronger yet,” teased Matt. Matt mentioned that he had a pull-up bar of his own that he used regularly, just a pipe that he and his dad had attached to the joists in the ceiling of their basement.

Robbie had a two mile course mapped out for such workouts. Running wasn’t nearly the workout that wrestling was, he figured, but if he went pretty hard for two miles he knew he’d get up a good sweat and work his heart, legs, and lungs. His dad had helped him measure it out using the family car’s odometer. His course took him out the back side of the neighborhood, across the railroad tracks and down the road. Basically, they measured a mile from the house and knew that by the time he ran back he'd have his two miles.

Monday's workout went off without a hitch. He got in the run, did some push-ups, sit-ups, and pull-ups, stretched out and then took a shower. Tuesday's run was a little more interesting. As Robbie jogged through the back side of the neighborhood he could see Jake Armstrong and a couple of his buddies hanging out on someone's front porch. Jake yelled out sarcastically, "Hey Robbie, we heard about you getting your picture in the paper. Come here and give us an autograph!"

Robbie figured they were at least half-joking and just laughed, waved, and kept running. By the time Robbie was moving past the house, Jake and his cronies had walked over to the home's gravel driveway. Jake the snake then yelled out, "So you won't sign an autograph, huh? Well what if I autograph your ass with this rock?" Jake then chucked a rock at Robbie and his friends quickly joined in. No real damage was done, but Robbie was dodging rocks until he was out of throwing distance. On his return trip Robbie wisely came back through a street farther down.

Practice started back up Friday with the team members happy to get back together and talk about what they'd gotten for Christmas. Robbie had gotten mostly clothes and a few DVD's and preferred talking about the tournament and the team photo in the newspaper. Everyone was still excited about the tournament championship. Coach Moore pitched in with the expression "Once a champion, always a champion."

Coach Destin made it clear that they had a week to get ready for their second and final holiday tournament, the Capital City Classic. One week after that they would be back in school and wrestling dual meets again. The "Classic" sounded like a tough event. Twelve teams would participate. One was actually from out of state, four from the state capital area, and the other seven were competitive teams from various parts of the state. Canady High School, Destin pointed out, had never actually won the championship at this prestigious event but had seen a lot of individual success in it.

Training progressed through the coming week and the team was excitedly looking forward to the upcoming challenge. Jeff Fencik had returned to train with his college team but Robbie, Matt, and now Floyd were getting in some extra workouts and looking sharp. The extra work was paying off for Robbie in that he was now routinely beating the team's 125-pounder Chris Farner, staying even with Floyd, and giving Matt a good match. He had beaten J.D. Maloney, the team's 135-pounder in a close practice match Wednesday.

On the day of the tournament routines were pretty predictable. Everyone knew by then what to bring, what music to listen to, what to eat or not eat, where they liked to sit on the bus, and who to hang out with. The team left before dawn broke for their 1 ½ hour drive to the state capital.

The Pirates wrestled hard throughout the tournament and finished up with mixed results. Last year's state championship team won the tournament followed by the out-of-state team in second place. Those two teams had dominated the team score, each advancing several wrestlers to the championship finals. The rest of the teams were much more evenly matched. Canady H.S. finished 4th out of the 12 teams in what amounted to an "All Star" event. Justin at 103 and Charles at 189 had won individual championships. Among Canady's other place winners Matt had placed fourth. Robbie had won two matches and lost two and failed to place. Gary at 112 and Artel at 145 had gone "0-2 and out," meaning that they had lost both of their matches. It was a tough event.

As usual, Coach Destin sat the team down at the completion of the tournament and summarized their day in the capital city. He pointed out that it was more fun to win, but that the experience of such a competitive field would help the team down the road in the Conference and Regional tournaments, and hopefully at State. "Win or lose, it's all good wrestling experience. We'll be a better team next week because of it," he said.

Robbie and Matt sat together on the bus trip home rehashing the day's events. This being a large event, Matt had earned a medal for his fourth place finish. He was still shaking his head over a couple mistakes in his semi-finals match that cost him a trip to the finals and at least second place. Robbie was frustrated too, since a close loss in his last match had cost him a shot at a medal. He agreed with Coach Destin, though, that he was getting valuable experience.

They drove past a construction site on the way out of town and Matt kidded him saying, “You’d better hope Jake the snake doesn’t see that pile of rocks over there. That’s a year’s supply to throw at your head!” Robbie gave Matt a shove and laughed it off. Matt laughed too and almost fell off the seat into the aisle. They both laughed at that.

Chapter 20 – The Meatball

One strange thing about going to school was that you were always looking forward to getting away from school. Always looking forward to the next break, whether it was Thanksgiving, Christmas, Easter, or summer. The strange thing, though, was that after you'd been out on break for a while you were looking forward to seeing your old friends and getting back to school. At practice Monday and Tuesday talk among the team members was about school starting back up Wednesday, and Friday night's conference match at Charles E. Harris High School.

The Harris Hawks were one of the Pirates long-time rivals. After practice Monday, Robbie, Matt, and Floyd were talking about the upcoming match while getting in a jog. Matt told Robbie that the Hawks always gave them a heckuva match but that A.L. Canady almost always managed to win somehow. Robbie said he hoped that continued to be true and asked if they knew anything about his opponent. Floyd said he'd seen his name in the newspaper but it didn't "ring a bell." That was probably good news, thought Robbie. Both Matt and Floyd's opponents would likely be returning starters.

Matt spoke up and said, "You know, all three of us have a good shot at winning Friday night." "That's right," said Floyd, "You and I saw our opponents last year and we can handle those guys and Robbie's guy didn't start last year." "I think Danny's going to have the toughest match," said Matt, and Floyd agreed. "Why's that," asked Robbie. "Danny has to wrestle "Meatball" Brown, their heavyweight. He won the conference championship last year." Matt laughed and said, "Floyd, tell him what you asked Meatball at the weigh-in last year." Robbie then said, "Yeah, what happened?" Floyd laughed and said, "Last year at the weigh-in I kept hearing his teammates call him Meatball, which you gotta figure is an odd thing to be calling someone. So I asked him why they called him that. Meatball laughed when I asked him and then said loudly, 'Cause I'm big, round, and Brown.'"

Several of Meatball's teammates had laughed when they heard that, and it was true. Meatball was fairly short but weighed about 270 pounds. He was barrel-chested and round but was very strong and his last name was Brown. So he was big, round, and Brown, like a meatball. "Yeah, Danny's a good heavyweight but he lost to Meatball every time last year," said Floyd, "I hope we've got the dual meet locked up before we get to heavyweight."

The three took turns practicing their favorite moves before finishing up with a takedown three-some and stretching out. Coach Destin was a proponent of the “KISS system,” or Keep It Simple, Stupid. Translated to wrestling that meant that you didn’t need to have 50 different moves that you were likely to score with but really just one or two from each position. They worked on a variety of moves in practice in order to be familiar enough with them to counter them. It was hard, however, to get real good at a lot of different moves; there just wasn’t enough time. Destin felt that offensively you should put most of your work into a few favorite holds. For Robbie that had become the ‘double-leg’ from his feet, the ‘cradle’ from the top, and the ‘roll’ from the bottom.

Robbie could hardly believe it, but it felt good to get back to classes on Wednesday. Yes, they were the same old hard desks to sit in for six hours a day but Robbie had friends in school and he liked most of his teachers, too. At practice that afternoon Robbie noticed that Coach Moore was spending most of his time working with Danny and his partner James back in the "heavyweight corner." There was no designated place for any of the weight classes to work out in the room but the big guys always seemed to end up in that corner. The lightweights, conversely, headed for the opposite corner, perhaps out of a concern for personal safety.

They were working on what Coach Moore was calling the "Meatball defense." Robbie had never seen Meatball wrestle so Matt explained, "Meatball is so short and powerful that he usually just drives in under the other heavyweight, locks up a 'bear hug,' and powers them over to their backs. I think Coach Moore is reminding Danny how to use his hands to fight off the Meatball. You definitely don't want to muscle around with that guy."

Later in practice when the team was working on moves from the bottom position, Robbie mentioned to Matt that Coach Moore was back there with Danny and James again and only working on 'rolls' from the looks of it. "Think about it," said Matt. "Your favorite move from bottom is a 'roll' but sometimes you get frustrated when some tall guy stretches out and you lose the leverage to roll him. Well, Meatball sure can't stretch out like that so a 'roll' might work on him. If Danny can hit it before he gets crushed, that is."

After school Friday Robbie, Matt, and Floyd checked weight and then started up a card game on the mat to relax and pass the time. Since the match was away it wouldn't be too long before they had to leave. In the meantime wrestlers checked their weights in the locker room and popped in and out of the wrestling room. J.D. Maloney came in and joined the card players to make it a foursome. A couple guys were running around the room in sweats trying to get that last fraction of a pound off.

Soon enough, Coach Destin was calling the team together for a few quick reminders and then it was off to the activity bus. Several wrestlers already had headphones on as others got into their usual bus routines. There was always some kidding around on the bus trips, but it was generally a serious, determined group on the way to a match. All hoped they would be a satisfied, relaxed group on the way back.

Upon their arrival, the team bus drove past a large lighted sign by the entrance which declared, "Charles E. Harris High School, Home of the Fighting Hawks." The team members filed off the bus, through the gym lobby and into the gym. The gym was unusual in that it had upper decks on both sides. On the left side, Matt could see large nets and other equipment upstairs. Apparently the athletic department had set up indoor batting cages up there.

The right upper deck was apparently the "wrestling room." It really wasn't a room since it was completely open to the gym, save for a railing above the bleachers on the upper level.

The Harris team members were in the process of bringing the mats down for the match. At most schools that would require rolling them up on the large tubes and moving them to the gym. Some schools didn't even use rollers but would get about ten guys and physically lift a whole mat section and just carry it! The Harris Hawks, however, were using a completely different method of moving the mats. Up in the upper deck several of their wrestlers would grab the end of a thirty-eight foot long mat section and drag it to the railing. There, they would lift the end and slide it over the top rail and pass it to several of their teammates who were standing on the top row of the bleachers. Those Hawks would then carefully walk down the bleachers thus sliding the mat section down to the gym floor with them. It looked like a giant, wide anaconda wriggling down a hill in search of prey.

The Pirate grapplers continued through the gym to the locker room in order to check weights before the actual weigh-in. Apparently, for every home match the Hawks had to slide all three mat sections down the bleachers and then reverse the process at the conclusion of the dual meet. Robbie mentioned to Matt his idea that the mat had looked like a huge anaconda and Matt replied that, "Yeah, a snake that big could eat all of us! What if one of those guys tripped on his way down the bleachers? He'd be in bad shape." "Right," said Robbie, "And I thought moving the mats with the rollers was hard!"

Once the dual meet started it must have appeared that both teams were politely taking turns claiming victories. Justin won easily at 103 pounds but then Gary lost at 112. Floyd won a close match at 119 but then Chris lost at 125. Noticing this trend Robbie thought to himself that, "It must be my turn to win" and set out to fulfill that plan. It was a good match for Robbie. The first he could recall in which he'd actually scored with all three of his favorite moves in the same match. Robbie had caught his opponent reaching for his head in the first period and used his hands to pop up his opponent's arms to set up his 'double-leg' takedown. It had worked just like in practice. Later in the period his Hawk opponent had attempted a 'switch' that Robbie failed to counter properly and it led to an escape. Robbie was ahead 2-1 at the end of the first period.

Robbie's opponent was pretty tough from the top position and "rode" him for over a minute. Robbie was never in any danger of being turned to his back but he was frustrated in his several scoring attempts. Late in the second period Robbie's hustle paid off. He hit another 'turn-in' looking for a 'roll' and his opponent, maybe getting a little tired, hadn't followed quite as well as before. Robbie caught the top man's leg with his foot and 'elevated' him over with his 'side roll.' His opponent bridged over to his stomach but Robbie scored two points for the reversal and held a 4-1 lead going into the last period.

Coach Moore shouted out to Robbie to "Look for your 'cradle'" as he got set on top for the third period. The Hawk had no interest in getting cradled and hit a 'stand-up' on the whistle. Robbie spent most of the next minute tripping his opponent back down to the mat only to have him hit another 'stand-up.' Robbie finally caught his opponent's foot after tripping him back down and picked the foot up realizing that his opponent couldn't stand up without a foot! From there he worked into a cross face and could hear Coach Moore's familiar refrain,

"Make him kiss his knee!" Robbie did in fact drive the bottom man's head to his knee and locked up his cradle. Fighting and kicking all the while, the Hawk was rocked to his back with the 'cradle' anyway and the referee dived to his stomach to look for a pin.

Two factors then came into play for the last forty seconds of the match. First of all, his opponent's kicking and twisting had kept Robbie from really planting him on both shoulders. Only one of the Hawk's shoulders was down and his twisting action wouldn't allow Robbie to get the other one down for the pin. The referee had counted out the five seconds necessary for a three-point near fall, however. The second factor, as Robbie discovered, was that despite his opponent's kicking and squirming he wasn't getting off his back. Robbie's grip was just too strong. The extra pull-ups were already paying off. He kept his grip until the buzzer sounded to end the period and the referee signaled, "Three, near fall." Robbie had won a solid 7-1 decision.

Momentum in the dual meet continued to swing back and forth. J.D. lost a close match at 135 pounds before Matt won solidly at 140. The team score stayed close all evening. Going into the final match of the night Canady held a five point lead over the Harris Hawks. The pressure was now on the heavyweights. Ordinarily the Pirates would have felt confident with a five point lead and their athletic heavyweight Danny Bozworth "stepping up to the plate." Tonight, though, Danny was a definite underdog to the fearsome Meatball, the returning conference champ.

Everyone in the gym probably realized that with a five point lead, Danny could actually lose his match by a decision (3 team points) and the Pirates would still win the dual meet by two points. A pin, however, scored <u>six</u> team points and a pin by

Meatball, which was a very real possibility, would win the dual meet for the Hawks. A good crowd was present for the meet and tension was at its peak as the final match approached.

Fans love the big guys. Even though the lightweights and middleweights are generally more active, most fans look forward to the heavyweights. There's just something about a big man going down hard, or at least the possibility of them going down hard that gets the fans excited. The home crowd Harris High School fans could just "smell" a come-from-behind victory as their champion Meatball Brown approached the scorers table to check in. Danny did the same. A Hawks fan stood up and yelled, "Pin him, Meatball!"

As the two heavyweights stepped to the center of the mat the home fans started chanting, "Meatball! Meatball! Meatball!" The noise level quickly rose as the chant echoed off the metal ceiling of the gym. On the referee's whistle an obviously pumped-up Meatball launched himself forward like a Sumo wrestler and drove Danny backwards off the mat. The referee blew his whistle signaling them out-of-bounds. Several Hawks fans booed Danny. The fans picked up the chant again, "Meatball! Meatball! Meatball!" Only three seconds had elapsed on the clock. Coach Destin yelled out, "Circle Danny, don't get shoved out!"

The referee again blew his whistle for wrestling to begin. Meatball again charged forward trying to drive up under Danny for his crunching 'bear hug.' Danny circled with him this time instead of backing up and used his hands to fight off Meatball's attack and keep him at arms length. Danny well knew that it would be a mistake to lock up and "muscle" with the Meatball and he had been coached all week to hand-fight and keep his opponent at arm’s length.

Meatball was clearly the stronger of the two and outweighed Danny by several pounds. Meatball was his nickname, but “Stump” would have been just as appropriate. He was short, stout, and well-muscled in the legs and shoulders. Danny, however, had the greater reach, a more athletic build and was a good wrestler in his own right. He was determined to "go the distance" for the team.

For the first minute Danny was able to hand-fight and circle effectively to keep it a scoreless bout. At that point they went out-of-bounds again and headed back to the center circle for a restart. The home crowd started chanting again, “Meatball! Meatball! Meatball!” Terrance Ellison’s parents were two of the team’s most supportive fans and they frequently were accompanied by Terrance’s Uncle Roscoe. Roscoe Ellison was frequently suspected of being just a little bit intoxicated at some of the events. This had never led to any problems, but was perhaps part of the reason he was such a “spirited” fan. As the Hawks fans concluded their latest chant of “Meatball! Meatball! Meatball!” Uncle Roscoe stood up, pointed in the direction of the Harris Hawks fans and yelled back, “We gonna smash your Meatball!” Robbie, on the bench, wondered for a moment if trouble was going to break out in the bleachers but Mrs. Ellison tugged on Roscoe's sleeve and he sat back down.

It’s not clear whether Meatball actually heard Roscoe Ellison, but on the next whistle he drove up under Danny and finally locked up his ‘bear hug.’ Not wanting to have to fight the hold from his back, Danny quickly turned his back to his opponent and fell to his stomach, giving up the two-point takedown instead of the pin. Meatball worked him over pretty good for the rest of the period while Danny conservatively just stayed off his back. The period ended with the score 2-0.

The second period started with Danny on top with hopes of breaking his opponent down and wearing him out for a while. Meatball was short and powerful. One thing about being short is that you don't have far to go to stand up. Meatball drove up quickly to his feet on the whistle and his powerful hips helped him pop out for an escape and one point. He was just too strong for Danny to hold onto. Meatball kept pressing the action realizing that he had to have the pin to win the dual meet for the Hawks. Conversely, Danny stayed with his strategy of circling and hand-fighting and largely frustrating the more powerful Meatball. At the end of the second period the Hawks heavyweight was still up 3-0.

Robbie turned to Matt at that point and said, "I think Meatball's slowing down a little bit.

What do you think?" Matt replied, "You may be right. He pins most of his opponents and usually doesn't have to go this hard. I think Danny can go the distance with him if he doesn't screw up." As the wrestlers got set for the third period the crowd got into it again, chanting "Meatball! Meatball! Meatball!" Danny took bottom position realizing that he had to stay off his back for two more minutes. Meatball took top determined to get the pin for himself and the team.

Danny hit a 'stand-up' on the whistle, or at least he tried one, before Meatball arm chopped him back down to the mat. Meatball then went to work trying to force a 'half nelson' but Danny kept his elbows in and worked back up to his knees. Throughout the first minute of the third period Meatball kept breaking Danny down to his stomach but in each case Danny was able to turn away from the 'half nelson' and work his way back to his knees. Eventually they went out-of-bounds on the Pirates side of the mat. Coach Moore called to Danny, "Hey, where's that roll we worked on?" The expression on Danny's face indicated that he was doing all he could just to "stay alive" out there. Dutifully though, on the next referee's start Danny tried a 'sit-out' and 'turn-in' but Meatball just knocked him back to his stomach. Danny worked back up to his knees once again and gave it another shot, 'sit-out,' 'turn-in,' and the tiring Meatball was a little slow countering this time. Danny athletically continued his 'turn-in' right up under his stocky opponent and rolled him over to his back.

The referee called out, "Two, reversal," and dived down to count for near fall points. Meatball struggled, then bridged forcibly back over to his stomach and started working up to his knees as the ref declared, "Three, near fall." Always a champion, Meatball fought up to his feet and out quickly for an escape to close the score to 5-4 in favor of Danny. Meatball was tired but had an "adrenaline rush" from the fear of losing and quickly forced the action. It was too late, though. As Danny fought him off with his hands and circled back to the center the buzzer sounded ending the match. The Pirate wrestlers and all their fans immediately stood and cheered. Roscoe Ellison was the loudest among them yelling, "Yeah! We smashed your Meatball!"

Chapter 21 – Ironwood

On Saturday, the day after the win over Harris High, Robbie was next door shooting some baskets with his friend Al when Matt drove up and honked his horn. Robbie didn't recognize the vehicle, a late model Jeep Cherokee. Floyd was sitting in the passenger seat. Matt seemed to be sporting an unusually large smile. "My parents just got it for me as a late birthday present," Matt beamed, "It's four years old but it runs like a champ." Matt was 16 and had had his driver's license for a few months.

"Hey, let's take it out for a spin," said Robbie. "I'm game," added Al. Floyd suggested that they play some 2-on-2 when they got back and Robbie countered, "Better yet, let's drive over to the park on Elm Street and play on a real court." Robbie and Al hopped in the back seat and they drove the several blocks to the park, all the time asking Matt questions about his new wheels.

Robbie said, "Hey, we could go off-roading in this thing!" Matt answered, "No, it's not the four-wheel drive model." "Oh," said Robbie, "what's it got under the hood?" Matt then said that it had the six cylinder 4.0 liter engine which, he said, gave it some good pick-up.

The jeep passed over the railroad tracks and the bridge over a small creek and into the park. There were trees in the park but the basketball court was in a cleared area not too far from the creek. Occasionally someone would make a really bad pass and the ball would end up in the creek.

The guys played some 2-on-2 and after the first game took a break and walked to the water fountain for a drink. Matt mentioned that they would have two more conference matches in the coming week, Tuesday and Friday. Floyd added, "Ironwood on Friday is going to be the tough one," and Matt replied, "You're right, but we'd better take 'em one at a time." They played another game and then headed home.

At practice Monday Coach Destin mentioned in his match summary that Robbie had done a good job holding onto his cradle despite his opponent's attempts at kicking out. Robbie felt pride that his coach had found something positive in his match and not just another mistake to correct. He mentioned to Matt that he was now doing at least 10 pull-ups every morning and evening and sometimes up to 12 and felt it was improving his grip and pulling strength. Matt agreed, saying, "With the human body it's 'use it or lose it.' The guys on this team are probably in better shape than anybody else in the school. I probably won't wrestle all my life, but I sure don't want to end up fat and lazy." Robbie agreed.

Coach Destin didn't mention anything about the match Friday with Ironwood High School. His whole focus was on Tuesday night's conference match with Farmington Central. With weight to make the next day, and not wanting to risk injury, the coaches put the team through a "drill practice." They did no "live" wrestling except for a few "live" situations for 15-20 seconds each. Mostly they just went drill, drill, drill from one move to another with only a water break midway through practice to catch a breath. Even without much "live" action it was a tough workout due to the constant, intense drilling.

Canady was a heavy favorite in the match against Farmington and it went off much as expected. Farmington won only four of the fourteen bouts as the Pirates rolled to a 42-15 victory. Canady H.S. won the JV match as well. Even the coaching staff could now concentrate on Friday night's home match with the Ironwood High Tigers. Coach Destin mentioned after the match that the conference championship usually went to either

Canady or Ironwood and this would be our first chance to prove that we were "top dog."

The intensity level at practice Wednesday and Thursday seemed to have been taken up a notch. What they worked on in practice was basically the same, but with the big match coming up the intensity of every drill and activity was increased. The seniors were constantly talking things up and reminding their teammates about the big match.

In a bit of comic relief, Justin pulled one of his stunts during Thursday's water break. He managed somehow to hang upside down from one of the pull up bars…by only his heels! Justin was a strong, little guy and had his legs flexed in some manner so that only the heels of his feet were hooked over the bar with his toes pointed up towards the ceiling. He was yelling, "Look I'm Spiderman!" and laughing. Charles was amused by the spectacle and called out, "Hey Justin, Kirsten

Dunst is out in the hall and she wants to kiss you!" Danny added, "Yeah, and that'll be the first time he's ever been kissed!" The fun ended when Coach Destin said, "Okay, break's over. Get a partner."

The regular season conference championship seemed to be boiling down to a three team race. From their tight win over Harris High and Meatball last week they knew the Hawks were tough. Canady had beaten Ironwood H.S. last year in both the regular season match and the conference tournament but both wins had been close. Ironwood hadn't wrestled Harris High yet and was still undefeated in conference matches. It shaped up to be a good one Friday night.

Just a couple months earlier "match day" had been a new and unique experience for Robbie. Now he was into a routine. Still excited about each match, he could relax more and prepare himself for the challenge ahead. The Ironwood match being at home gave the team members a little more free time. Robbie and a couple of the guys hopped in Matt's Cherokee and headed to the Quick-Pick to get some snacks. Then it was back to school to check weight. Some of the basketball players were shooting in the gym before leaving for their game. They watched the shoot-around for a while and then decided to play cards in the wrestling room. On the way out of the gym Matt asked Robbie, "Do you know why basketball is bad for you?" "Is this a joke?" asked Robbie. "Come on," repeated Matt, "Why is basketball bad for you?" "I don't know, why?" replied Robbie. "Because you end up with a 'basketball head,'" answered Matt, "hard on the outside and empty on the inside." Robbie chuckled, "That's pretty good, Matt."

The match against Ironwood didn't start out so funny. Justin would have the first match, as usual, after the National Anthem and the cross the mat introductions. All the wrestlers were introduced over the loudspeaker before the meet started, shaking hands at the center of the mat. Justin, who was having a great year at the 103 pound weight got caught on his heels and was taken down in the first period. He later got a reversal and tied it up 2-2 going into the second period.

Justin got an escape in the second period but neither wrestler could score a takedown and Justin had a narrow 3-2 lead going into the third period. Matt said Justin was a strong favorite in the match but that just an escape would tie it up for the Tiger wrestler. Justin got a leg ride in and was tying up his opponent pretty good. He finally turned him to his back for a two point near fall with a 'Jacobs' on the head, basically a 'cross-face' and ended up winning a hard-fought decision 5-2.

At 112, Gary wasn't one of the team's strongest wrestlers but he was better than his opponent and earned a 6-2 win. A.L. Canady was looking pretty good at that point. Floyd and Chris both lost in the next two matches, however, and the dual meet was tied up going into Robbie's match.

"Even more pressure," Robbie thought but he was focused in and ready to go. He checked in at the scorers table and then jogged to the center of the mat intent on tying up his opponent right away and getting the first takedown. It didn't work out that way. Robbie liked to tie up hard with his opponent after the whistle started the match. He often shot his 'double-leg' takedown from that position, and tying up hard also helped him get rid of the "butterflies" he had at the beginning of every match. Unfortunately, his opponent liked the tie-up position as well. Soon after the initial tie-up his opponent had Robbie's arm trapped and shot under him with a 'fireman's carry' takedown. Over his shoulder Robbie went and he soon found himself bridging off his back and down 4-0 in the match score. Robbie managed an escape later in the period and they went back to wrestling on their feet. Robbie was wary of his opponent's 'fireman's carry' now but couldn't score himself and the first period ended 4-1.

Robbie chose the down position in the second period hoping for a reversal to tighten up the score. He got pretty close to rolling his opponent twice and the Ironwood coach yelled, "Cut him" from his team bench. At that point, Robbie's opponent just let him go for an escape and they went back to wrestling from the standing position. Again, neither wrestler could gain a takedown and they went into the third period with Robbie in the top position but down in the score 4-2.

Robbie fought hard to keep his opponent down on the mat where he could lock up his 'cradle.' His opponent kept hitting 'stand-ups' apparently satisfied to just increase his lead by one point. On his fourth attempt the Ironwood wrestler finally managed to clear his hips after his 'stand-up' and escaped increasing his lead to 5-2. Now needing both a takedown and a near fall to win the match, Robbie immediately attacked his opponent. Having to almost chase him across the circle, Robbie tied up again and hoped for an opening. In his haste, Robbie made the mistake of walking right into his opponent and the Tiger shot his ‘fireman’s carry’ under Robbie for another takedown. No back points this time but the damage was done. Robbie managed an escape before time ran out but lost 7-3.

Robbie shook hands with his opponent and was still shaking his head in disbelief as he walked off the mat. His teammates were patting him on the back and saying “good match” but it didn’t seem too good. He felt like he had been ready to go and had hustled but none of the breaks had gone his way. Maybe the Tiger wrestler had made his own breaks?

J.D. Maloney lost the next match to make it four Ironwood wins in a row. That hadn't happened all season and the attitude on the bench seemed to change some, a sort of tightness was developing. Perhaps sensing this, Coach Destin got up and started walking behind the team bench patting guys on the head or back and saying, "Let's get it going again guys," and "This is our mat fellas. Let's wrestle like a bunch of Pirates!" Coach Moore was patting Matt on the back and telling him to "Go get one for the team!"

Matt was determined to do just that. Psyched up, he almost immediately scored a takedown and went to work from the top position. He turned his opponent for a near fall, but got a little "high" on him going for the pin and gave up an escape. Matt went right back after him and scored another takedown and ended the first period with a 6-1 lead.

The Ironwood wrestler chose bottom in the second period and immediately attempted a 'stand-up' for an escape. Matt, however, picked him up and brought him right back down. The Tiger 140-pounder landed on his left side and fairly hard. Somebody on the opposing bench yelled "Slam!" but the referee didn't think so. It was a firm but clean throw. As his opponent rolled to his stomach, Matt grabbed his wrist with his right hand and a 'half nelson' with his left and rotated out to his left attempting to drive the Tiger over to his back.

The Ironwood wrestler attempted to stick his right foot out to block Matt's action but Matt drove him over anyway. As the bottom man attempted to bridge the home fans began to chant, "Pin! Pin! Pin!" Initially only the shoulder closest to Matt was down but he adjusted his position, clamped down, and drove him down to the second shoulder. The referee counted two seconds and slapped the mat, calling out "Pin!"

The six points for the pin tightened up the team score considerably. The Pirates won three decisions in the next four matches but the lone Ironwood win was by pin. As such, Canady H.S. had a three point lead going into the 189 pound class. Word on the bench was that both Charles and Danny were solid favorites to win tonight while James at 215 was not. All the Pirates had to do to insure victory was to win two of the last three matches and the odds were in their favor. Things were looking good for another close win over Ironwood.

Charles took a lot of pride in being a team captain and was determined to do his part for a team victory. His opponent, a sophomore up from last year's JV was athletic, maybe even stronger than Charles but not nearly as experienced. Charles worked him over like a pro. The Ironwood H.S. wrestler had a lot of fight in him but couldn't stop Charles' smooth offense. Charles was up 9-2 going into the third period and, aiming for a pin, chose the top position.

On the whistle, the bottom man hit a 'switch' but Charles did a 'shoulder drive' and knocked him down to his stomach. Fighting inside for hand control, Charles managed to lock up a 'half nelson' and quickly ran out to the side to drive him over. The home fans again took up the chant of "Pin! Pin! Pin!" The Canady H.S. wrestlers had all been coached to take the time to get a 'half nelson' locked up correctly before going for the pin. That is, to get the elbow locked behind the opponent's neck and to keep your butt down while driving the bottom man over.

In his rush for the pin Charles forgot that basic lesson and had his butt up too high as he drove his opponent over to his back. The bottom man naturally bridged as he was being turned. Charles realized too late that his position was too high. He lost his balance as his Tiger opponent bridged up high, and due to the bottom man's strength he was able to continue the motion and roll Charles over to his own back. The climate in the gym immediately changed 180 degrees! The chant of "Pin! Pin! Pin!" suddenly died out and a clamor arose among the visitors.

Could the sophomore from Ironwood pin the Canady captain? Charles was a broad-shouldered athlete and wide shoulders, while strong, are hard to get off the mat. His opponent was young, but very strong and instantly rose to the occasion. "Here's my chance!" he must have been thinking. Charles struggled mightily but he was locked up tight with plenty of time on the clock. With 30 seconds left the pin was called and all those from Ironwood, wrestlers and fans, leaped to their feet and cheered.

The Tigers won as expected at 215 to go ahead 27-21 going into the heavyweight match. Canady H.S. would have to have a pin at heavyweight to even tie the score. Danny gave every effort for six minutes, beating a credible adversary 5-2, but never was able to turn his cautious opponent to his back. Ironwood H.S. won the dual meet 27-24.

Chapter 22 – The Pep Rally

At the beginning of Monday's practice Coach Destin sat the team down to review the Ironwood loss. He said that he knew that it was a tough loss for all of us to take because we had made a good effort to win. He also pointed out that when the team won we all won together, and when the team lost that was also shared. A few sets of eyes shifted over to Charles when he said that, since his upset loss had put the team at a serious disadvantage. "No one wrestler can win a dual meet," Destin went on, "and no one wrestler can lose one. Seven Pirate wrestlers lost Friday night," he continued, "and if **any** of them had won, the team would have won. Also, if any of our wrestlers that won a decision had scored a pin, then the meet would have ended in a tie."

Coach Destin then, as usual, started going through the weight classes mentioning, from his match notes, both positives and negatives for each wrestler. For the negatives he had the wrestler practice a correction back in the corner with his partner, or in some cases, had Coach Moore work through the problem with them.

When Destin got to the 130-pound class he pointed out that Robbie had lost 7-3 and that six of those seven points had come off of his opponent's 'fireman's carry.' "This is something you've had problems with before and it's often hard for a rookie to learn how to feel it coming and stop it." He then looked at Coach Moore and said, "Coach, all six points came after Robbie tied up with the guy and pushed in. Go work with him some on setting up his 'double' without a tie-up." Coach Moore nodded at both Robbie and Matt to move back to the corner and first showed Robbie how his hard tie-up and pushing was helping set up his opponent's 'fireman's carry.' Then he reviewed two set-ups that Robbie really already knew, the 'pop-up' and the 'snap and go.'

"Look, you might wrestle this guy again in the Conference Tournament and if you take that 'fireman's carry' away from him you might beat him," said Coach Moore. "You've got a good 'double,' he continued, "Get in the habit of either snapping the top of your opponent's head and then shooting under him when he looks up or, if he reaches for **your** head, just pop his arms up with your hands and go under him. Take a few reps with Matt and let me see what you've got." Robbie did what he was told and hit a few 'doubles' with each of the two set-ups. "You see," said Moore, "you can get your shot without the tie-up. Give it a try that way."

When Coach Destin got to the 189-pound match he very fairly pointed out that there had been a likely 12-point turnaround at that weight class.

Charles looked like he was going to get a pin and six points for Canady H.S. and ended up getting pinned and losing six instead. Charles shook his head and said, "I'm sorry Coach, I got in a hurry and blew that one." "Thanks Charles," said Destin, "but no apology is necessary. Every man in this room knows you put out a good effort every match. At the same time, we don't want to see anyone getting pinned with their own moves. Let's take a look at what went wrong." He then drilled the entire team on one of their basic skills, running a 'half nelson' correctly and keeping the butt down while driving the opponent over.

After finishing with the individual coaching, Destin walked over to the bulletin board and pointed to the team's wrestling schedule declaring that, "We've got four conference dual meets left. If we win out and Harris High beats Ironwood next week we could still finish the regular season in a 3-way tie for the regular season conference championship. If not, there's still the Conference Tournament. Since all eight conference schools will be there the same day, that's really the title we're shooting for." "Let's go for it guys!" said someone in the back of the room and several more added, "Yeah!"

Matt, Robbie, and Floyd got in a run after practice and then hit some moves. Robbie concentrated on the set-ups for the 'double-leg' that he'd worked on with Coach Moore earlier. "In my match tomorrow night," said Robbie, "I think I'm going to try to go with no tie-ups and just shoot under the guy like Coach said." "Right," said Matt, "Just get in a good stance and take a shot off one of your set-ups."

Tuesday's match was at home versus Plateburg High School. Their nickname was the Patriots and they showed up in red, white, and blue uniforms. Their uniforms looked better than most of their wrestlers, however, and Canady H.S. cruised to a 35-15 conference win. Floyd, Robbie, and Matt all won. Robbie tried out his new standing strategy of not using his favored hard tie-ups but rather getting set in a good stance and looking for an opening. His opponent, as it turned out, did like to tie up so when he did Robbie just pushed him away. When his opponent tried again to reach for Robbie's head and tie up, Robbie anticipated it and shoved his opponent's arms up and shot under him for his 'double-leg' takedown. This caught the Patriot wrestler leaning in and Robbie scored a clean takedown.

Robbie rode him out in the first period for a 2-0 lead. Starting from the bottom in the second period, the Plateburg wrestler escaped. The Patriot then tried to tie up Robbie's head again only to have Robbie shoot under him for another 'double-leg' takedown. Robbie entered the third period on the bottom and leading 4-1. The top man got a leg ride in on Robbie early in the period and it took Robbie about forty seconds to kick out of it. Robbie then hit a 'sit-out' and immediately tried his 'turn-in roll.' It worked just like in practice and he rolled the Patriot grappler over to his back. His opponent still had some fight left in him but Robbie was able to adjust, clamp down, and finally get the pin. The home crowd cheered and Robbie then had one of the great feelings in sports, having his hand raised by the referee after a tough match.

The shortest match of the night occurred at 189 pounds where Charles, still upset with Friday night's match, wanted desperately to take out his frustration on somebody and that somebody was the poor guy from Plateburg. Charles charged at his opponent on the whistle only to have him back out of bounds and get warned for stalling by the ref. On the restart the Patriot tried to hold his ground, if only briefly, and Charles headlocked him to the mat and scored a pin in less than thirty seconds. Charles got a big cheer. His teammates and the home crowd knew he was coming off a tough loss.

After Tuesday night's win, practice was pretty upbeat on Wednesday and seemed to go by quickly. At the end of practice Coach Destin sat the team down for announcements and mentioned that the team would travel Friday night to another conference team, Millsville. All the remaining matches were in their conference. He pointed out that Millsville's nickname was the "Moccasins" and joked, "Be careful with those Moccasins Friday night. They've got a nasty bite!"

The second announcement was, "In case you haven't heard, Ironwood beat Harris High last night so if they continue winning they will capture the regular season conference championship and if we keep winning we'll finish second. We want to keep taking these matches one at a time, but a good long-range goal would be to win the Conference Tournament. It's at Ironwood H.S. this year so it would be sweet revenge for their win over us here. There's an old expression in sports, 'Turnabout is fair play.'" "Is winning the tournament our 'destiny' Coach?" kidded Terrance. "That's right," added Charles, "Destin said it, so it's our 'destiny.'"

Coach smiled then pointed out that there was plenty of wrestling left this season but obviously some athletes had better records than others. "That's the nature of sports," he said. "Every time one man or team wins, someone else takes a loss." He pointed out that every athlete had made contributions to the team during the season and that those who might finish with a losing record were still valued members of the team. "That reminds me of one of our former Canady High wrestlers, Preston

Shultz." Matt elbowed Robbie and whispered, 'Story time." "Preston had wrestled for the middle school and finished with a losing record," said Destin. "He came out for the high school team in the ninth grade and just wasn't very physical, but he tried hard. He had another losing season that year but he knew he liked to wrestle and liked being on the team and came back out again as a sophomore. Even with a couple of years experience, he still finished with a losing record again as a sophomore. Really, he was happy to have made the varsity line-up and kept hustling and fighting through the losses."

"At the beginning of his junior season Preston's mother walked up to me and asked a question. She had been suffering through the years of losses and an occasional exciting win with her son and she asked me, 'Coach, is Preston EVER going to have a winning season?' I told her yes, that his hustle and experience would start to pay off. That junior season was pivotal for Preston and he finished with a winning record for the first time. He won the conference championship before he graduated! So, for you guys that aren't quite where you'd like to be yet, hang in there. Winning will be that much sweeter for you later."

At the beginning of practice on Thursday, Coach Destin mentioned that there would be a pep rally during the last class period on Friday and that we would be taking part in it. That sounded like fun to Robbie whose only previous experience with pep rallies was from up in the bleachers. Practice went pretty normally. They drilled their moves and counters a lot getting ready for their upcoming match at Oak City High School.

The main announcement at the end of practice detailed the pep rally and what to expect. "We've got the pep rally because the basketball team has a home game tomorrow night but all of our athletes get introduced," said Destin. He then explained that the cheerleaders would start things off with some cheers and routines. Then the swimming teams would be introduced as they walked in from the gym lobby, before sitting in the bleachers. The JV wrestlers would then do the same except the last four introduced would then roll out a section of wrestling mat from the end of the gym. The varsity starters would then use it during their introductions, then roll it back up to make way for the basketball teams.

Coach Destin explained that many in the student body had never seen a wrestling match so we would at least show them a few takedowns. During introductions pairs of starters would each hit a move on the mat section in the center of the gym and then move over to the bleachers. "Cool," said Floyd. "That'll be all right," nodded Matt and

Robbie said, "I hope I don't screw up in front of all those people!" As much as possible, the wrestlers would each hit different takedowns to add a little variety and he went down through the line-up designating what takedown each man would demonstrate. Charles, for example, would get to hit a 'headlock' while Robbie was stuck with a simple 'double-leg,' which was fine with him.

The coach actually lined up the starters in the room for a run-through so they would know what to expect the next day in the gym. The starters were all lined up in order of weight class with one exception, he had Justin the 103-pounder at the end of the line with Danny the 260-pound heavyweight. He explained that for a little comic relief Danny was to let Justin throw him with a headlock. "People won't be expecting that," predicted Destin.

Each pair of wrestlers practiced being introduced and then jogging to the center and hitting heir takedown once each. Then the Justin/Danny show started. Coach Destin had Danny get down on one knee and instructed Justin to stand in front of him and make his body stiff as a rail. Danny was told to grab Justin by the back of the neck and the top of his thigh like a 103-pound barbell. "Okay Justin, now keep your body stiff and lean back into Danny," said the coach. Justin did this and Danny then leaned Justin back against his head and picked him up like a barbell. "All right," said Destin, "Now stand up Danny and don't drop him." "Yeah, don't drop him!" yelled Justin.

Danny was now on his feet with Justin's back laying across the top of his head. He was still holding Justin's neck and thigh. "Now Danny," said Coach, "See if you can press him up towards the ceiling." With a little bend of his knees and a grunt, Danny pushed up on the human barbell and locked his arms out. "Okay, now" said Destin, "see if you can walk across the room with him." Danny started to do so and Justin wiggled nervously and Danny had to drop him, to his feet fortunately. "Hey, quit wiggling," accused Danny. "All right, all right, let's try it again," said Coach.

There was excitement in the air at school on Friday since most of the students looked forward to the pep rally. The majority had an interest in the cheerleaders and athletic teams and **everybody** liked getting out of class. An announcement came during the last period for students to move to the gym for the pep rally and the halls were soon clogged with the mass of humanity. It looked like a cattle drive and the "herd" gradually worked its way down the hallways and into the bleachers of the gym. The wrestling team met in the wrestling room to get organized and avoid being trampled in the hallway.

Coach Destin checked to see that all were present and repeated the details to the team. Once the student body had cleared the halls the wrestlers joined the other athletes waiting in the gym lobby to be introduced. The cheerleaders were soon leading chants and had taken the liberty of rolling out the wrestling mat section themselves as a safer area to perform their stunts. Half of the varsity basketball players had their own ball out in the lobby and were huddled up as their coach was explaining the couple of drills they would perform to amuse the fans.

As expected, the boys and girls swim teams were introduced first and then the JV wrestlers. Gary and Floyd were the first two varsity wrestlers introduced. They jogged to the mat in the center of the gym and then Gary hit a ‘single-leg’ and Floyd got back up and hit an ‘arm drag.’ Robbie was teamed with Chris and thought to himself as he jogged out, “Don’t trip on the edge of the mat!” He didn't. Chris hit a 'fireman's carry,' a move all too familiar to Robbie, and then Robbie demonstrated his 'double-leg.' The other introductions went routinely enough.

Out in the lobby, and out of sight of the student body, Danny had lifted the now stiff Justin up on his head like a barbell as they had practiced. On cue, Danny stepped through the gym door sideways to avoid banging Justin's head and couldn't extend his arms up yet because of the height of the doorway. As Danny stepped through the door with his 103-pound cargo on his head a loud "Oooh!" was heard throughout the gym followed by a second "“Oooh!" when he turned towards the mat and pressed Justin up over his head. Justin, this time, lay perfectly rigid not wanting to be dropped on the rock maple floor of the gym! Danny marched methodically to the center of the mat and then dropped Justin down to his feet.

Looking much like David and Goliath the two wrestlers tied up and the crowd roared at the sight of little Justin apparently throwing the 260-pound heavyweight head over heels! There was a collective "Whooo!" in the crowd and some immediate laughter as everyone realized the prank.

The match that night at Millsville wasn't quite as much fun as the pep rally, but it was close enough for most. The Pirates claimed another conference win and were wrestling well with the Conference Tournament just two weeks away. The team won 37-19 but Robbie didn't fare so well, coming up on the short end of a 4-3 decision. He had locked up his 'cradle' in the third period with the score tied at 3-3 and was fighting to turn his opponent to his back. He had rushed it, gotten out of position, and his opponent had managed to grab his leg and almost reversed him. The resulting one point escape ended up being the difference in the match. "Rookie mistake," Robbie was thinking as his opponent's arm was raised. Once he had cooled off over on the bench, Matt leaned over and teased him saying, "You got bit by that Moccasin, didn't you?"

Robbie's parents had followed the team bus back from Millsville and picked him up outside the gym entrance. His parents had attended every match, home and away since Christmas. Robbie sat silently in the back seat while his parents discussed the match. Halfway home his mother looked over her shoulder and said, "Awful quiet back there." "I don't feel too good," replied Robbie. "You're not coming down with something are you," asked his mom. "No, I just don't feel too good about the match. I coulda beat that guy tonight. I just made a couple more stupid mistakes!"

His father spoke up saying, "Well I'm proud of you, son. I know you're frustrated because it was a close loss, but we like the way you're trying hard and getting better and we just feel like you've come a long way." "Thanks dad," Robbie said, "but it still stinks to lose one at the end like that."

"Robbie, it hurts because you care," said his mom, "We're glad you have that kind of pride in yourself." Robbie sat silently soaking in these new thoughts. His dad spoke up again, "Robbie, let me ask you a couple questions. First of all, when you first went out for the wrestling team back in November did you even think that you'd be starting for the varsity this year?" "No dad, you've got me there. I was just hoping to make the JV team," said Robbie. "Okay, second question," continued his father, "When school started last August were you even planning to be **on** the wrestling team?" Robbie finally smiled and admitted that he wasn't even thinking about it when school started. "Well," concluded his dad, "Sounds like you're way ahead of the game then." Robbie had to agree. Just trying out for the team had to be one of the best decisions he'd ever made on his own. Suddenly the night didn't seem so dark.

Robbie's dad headed for the bathroom when they got home while Robbie and his mom hung up their coats. "I want you to know that I appreciate you and dad coming to all these matches, particularly the away ones," he said. "I'm sure it's a lot of trouble and I appreciate the support."

"Robbie, you're our son," said his mom, "and we enjoy coming to the matches. Your dad, in particular, has made friends with a few of the other fathers and it seems like all he's got on his mind is the next match. And another thing," she continued, "have you noticed that your dad has cut way back on his drinking?" Robbie hadn't really thought of it, but yes dad was now only having an occasional beer now and then. He hadn't seen him drunk for over a month. "Your dad used to drink too much sometimes because money's usually tight around here and his boss puts a lot of pressure on him at work. He was trying to get those frustrations off his mind. Now I think he's not worrying about those things as much because he's looking forward to seeing you wrestle your next match." "Darn," thought Robbie, "How about that."

Chapter 23 – Jake the Snake

During Robbie's freshman year he had not been involved in any school activities and he had found high school, well, boring. This year he got up in the morning actually looking forward to going to school. He enjoyed interacting with his friends on the wrestling team, and practice and the matches gave him something to look forward to. Before school on Monday he was hanging out in the hallway talking to Matt. Robbie was telling him that they needed to keep getting in their extra workouts with the Conference Tournament the following week. "Yeah," said Matt, "Keep working on your favorite moves and make them work in these last two dual meets."

About that time Jake Armstrong was making his way down the hallway from behind Robbie and purposely bumped into him pretty hard as he went by. "Hey, watch yourself," laughed Jake, "You're gettin' in my way!"

Jake continued down the hall. “Man, that guy’s a real jerk!” commented Matt. “Yeah,” said Robbie, “but at least you don’t have to live near the guy.” The warning bell rang and both boys headed on to class.

The team had a home match Tuesday night and an away match Friday that week, with only the Conference Tournament Saturday of the following week. Floyd, Robbie, and Matt got in a run in the hallways after practice. While jogging down the back hall Robbie said, “You know we’re like the ‘Three Musketeers’ – ‘All for one and one for all!’” “I don’t know,” said Matt laughing, “I don’t remember any black Musketeer!” “Okay, okay,” said Floyd, “Well I’m just the man to integrate the group.” All three chuckled at that thought.

After the run the three took turns practicing their favorite moves with Robbie concentrating on his ‘double-leg,’ ‘cradle,’ and ‘roll.’ Matt helped him some with the defense for the 'fireman's carry,' his frequent weakness. "You know Robbie," said Floyd, "If you win both of these last two conference matches you'll go into the tournament next week as the #3 seed. That's pretty good for a rookie." "That's right," Matt added, "then if you can beat just one higher seeded wrestler you'd be in the finals." "That medal in the Christmas tournament felt great," answered Robbie. "If I can just medal again I'll be pretty satisfied." "Third would be good for a rookie," agreed Floyd, "but don't sell yourself short." "And don't take anybody for granted either," added Matt. Robbie thought to himself that he didn't need to worry about being overconfident.

They had their last home match of the season Tuesday night, hosting the Spartans of East Springfield. It was "Senior Night" and each senior on the team was called to the scorers table along with his parents and each mother was presented a single rose by the athlete. Cross-the-mat introductions were then held, the captains were called to the center for the toss of the coin, and then the wrestling started.

It was a good match for the Pirates as they defeated the visiting Spartans 32-14. The "Three Musketeers" all won. It was an important win for Robbie. Not so much for the toughness of his opponent, who really wasn't too tough, but to get his confidence back after Friday's loss. He felt that he not only won, but performed well without any mistakes. As always, it was a great feeling to have his arm raised after the win and to then, more relaxed, sit on the bench and cheer on his teammates. Matt was warming up behind the bench but walked over to Robbie and joked, "After that Moccasin 'bit' you last week I was worried that this Spartan would 'stab' you with his sword!" "No worries," he replied, "Pirates are tougher than Moccasins and Spartans!"

In English class the next morning Robbie was having trouble concentrating as Mr. Long explained that they would be beginning a new unit on ancient Greek literature. To Robbie, the word "ancient" generally referred to anything that had happened before he was born, so his mind was wandering back to Tuesday night's match. At that point Mr. Long said something that caught Robbie's attention, "Athletics was very important to the ancient Greeks. In fact, many of the Greek statues displayed in museums and art galleries today were sculpted in honor of champion athletes. We'll be reading some Plato, for example, and before he became a famous philosopher, and Robbie you're going to like this, he was a champion wrestler." Robbie's head immediately popped up and his interest captured. "And Robbie," he went on, "we'll also be reading about the funeral games for Patroklas in the Iliad including the wrestling match between Ajax and Odysseus." Billy in the front row spoke up asking who won the match, to which Mr. Long replied, "I'm going to let you find that out yourself in tonight's reading."

In the locker room that afternoon Robbie mentioned to Matt that he had a homework assignment that night that he was actually looking forward to. "Oh yeah, what's that?" asked Matt as he finished lacing up his shoes. "According to Mr. Long, there's a wrestling match between Ajax and somebody in our Literature book that we have to read about." "Ajax doesn't have to wrestle 'Meatball' does he?" joked Matt. "That's not too likely but I'll have to get back to you on that one," replied Robbie.

Robbie beat Matt to practice on Thursday. Matt came in and sat next to him on the mat and asked, "So, how did the match come out?" "What match?" replied Robbie. "You know, the match with the mighty Ajax and the other guy," answered Matt. "Oh yeah, it was pretty good," replied Robbie. "They were going at it real hard when this guy Odysseus trips Ajax and throws him right on his back. Then they get back to their feet and are really going after it again but nobody's scoring so this fellow Achilles steps in and calls it a draw." "A draw," complains Matt, "after that Odysseus threw him right on his back? I'd like to have some words with the referee on that one!" "Too late now," said Robbie, "the referee's been dead for over two thousand years!"

Friday was both the team's last regular season match and last away match. They were wrestling at Platt County High School, home of the Panthers. As the team walked through the gym towards the locker room they could see a huge painting of a panther spread across the end wall of the gym. "Hey Floyd," kidded Matt, "maybe you should be going to school here. You could be a 'black' panther!" "Yeah, you're just a funny guy," replied Floyd, shaking his head but smiling a little.

The Pirates were again the better team and prevailed 33-19. Floyd and Robbie both had solid wins. Matt won too, but had a scare. Matt was winning 8-2 late in the 3rd period when his opponent, in desperation, threw a legal 'headlock.' He caught Matt off-balance and threw him right on his back. Matt managed to continue the momentum and roll over to his stomach and lost only the two points for the takedown, winning the match 8-4. Later on the bench Matt shook his head and said, "I'd better learn that lesson and stay awake the whole six minutes." "You're just lucky you weren't out there with me," said Floyd, "being a black panther I would've gone for the throat and kept you on your back!" "Better today than next week," said Robbie. "You're right about that," said Matt, "No screw-ups at the tournament next week."

After the match Coach Destin sat the team down for a meeting in the locker room saying, "Boys, it's time to change our focus. Since the Ironwood H.S. loss we've taken 'em one at a time and won four straight conference meets to finish the season strong. Good job." Heads nodded in agreement. "Now it's time to focus on the 'three G's,'" he said. Robbie glanced at Matt with a look of curiosity but Matt just shrugged his shoulders. Destin continued, "Next week we need Good academics, Good training, and on Saturday a Good performance. Congratulations and have a good weekend. See you Monday ready to go." On their way out Matt said to Robbie, "If the weather's okay this weekend I'll give you a call and we can get together for a run." "Sounds good," Robbie replied.

There was a cold rain Saturday most of the day but Sunday proved to be much nicer. Matt called Robbie about getting a run in together and maybe watching some TV afterwards. Robbie suggested he get up with Floyd. If Floyd could come he would get Al next door and they could play some 2-on-2 down at the park again. "Sounds like a plan," said Matt. "I'll bring over my DVD of 'Rocky' and we'll watch it after the game. That ought to get us 'psyched up' for the tournament if anything will."

Robbie waited for Matt and Floyd over at Al's house. When they saw the Jeep pull into the driveway they piled in and headed for the park. They 'shot for teams' and Robbie and Al teamed up but managed to lose the first game 21-17. They needed a break and headed over to the water fountain talking about whether to switch or keep the same teams. Al said, "That was a good game. The sides we've got are pretty even." Floyd added, "The way I'm shooting today you'd have to get Dwayne Wade to win a game!" "Fat chance!" Robbie retorted. In reality, none of them were exceptional basketball players but they had fun and got in a good workout.

Halfway through the second game Matt took the ball out at the top of the "key" and looking beyond the court said, "Oh Christ, don't look now but here comes Jake the snake!" The other three looked anyway and, sure enough, Jake and his two buddies were walking their way, cigarettes in hand. "Maybe we oughta just play over at my house," said Al. Floyd replied, "It's a public park isn't it?"

Jake and his cronies seemed content to just stand off to the side of the basketball court, smoke heir cigarettes, and make insulting comments, especially after a missed shot. “You guys stink!” said one. “My little sister coulda made that shot!” said another. Al repeated his suggestion that they ust play in his driveway, commenting, “We don’t need to take their crap.” Matt spoke up saying, “No, Floyd’s right. It’s a public park and they’re not running us out of it. Anyway, they’ll get tired of this mess and go bother somebody else.” “I don’t know Matt,” said Al, “these guys play pretty rough sometimes.” “Maybe so, but at four against three they won’t like the odds. They’re just running their mouths.”

That may have been true, but a few minutes later a bad pass went out-of-bounds over by Jake and his boys. Robbie went over to retrieve the ball and Jake, looking as cocky as possible, said to him “I told you about that lousy black boy of yours and here you go bringin’ him here to my park.” “It’s a public park, Jake" said Robbie as he walked to the ball. Jake quickly stepped toward the ball and kicked it down the incline into the creek. It was a shallow creek so the ball wasn't going anywhere, but it was an obvious insult and angered Robbie enough to yell, "Why do you have to be so stupid, Jake?" That wasn't the best thing to say to Jake. With his history of doing poorly at school, being called stupid got him "hot" very quickly. Robbie was headed toward the creek to retrieve the ball but Jake stepped in front of him and shoved him in the chest. "Hey, who ya callin' stupid?" he yelled in Robbie's face.

Jake probably outweighed Robbie by 40 pounds and enjoyed throwing his weight around. The force of the blow was almost enough to knock him down, particularly since he hadn't expected it, but Robbie managed to maintain his balance. Going one-on-one with Jake was something that all of the ıeighborhood kids had worried about through the ɿears and all were eager to avoid. Without any ;orethought, Robbie shoved Jake back saying, "Lay ɔff, I'm just gonna get our ball!" Only weighing a .ittle over 130 pounds there wasn't nearly as much force in Robbie's shove and it didn't move Jake an inch.

"This could turn into a brawl real quick," Matt said to Floyd, "think we should step in?" "Not yet," replied Floyd, "Let's see how it plays out." "Punch him Jake!" yelled one of the cronies. Robbie had no interest in fighting anyone, particularly not Jake the snake but things were happening faster than he could think them through. Jake was immediately right back in Robbie's face and shoved him again, yelling "Shove me will ya? I'll show you, ya little asshole!" Things were going downhill fast so Robbie took a step backwards saying, "Look Jake I'm not looking for any trouble. I'm just going to get the ball."

Robbie started to step around Jake towards the creek but Jake stepped right in front of him again and popped him hard in the chest with the heels of both hands saying, "You ain't gonna get crap until I'm finished with you!" As a reflex action Robbie shoved him back again and then out of the corner of his left eye saw Jake's right fist coming, only too late. The fist crashed into the left side of Robbie's jaw and buckled his knees. There was an immediate rush of pain and the sight of Jake's ugly face scowling at him and taunting, "Put 'em up you asshole, I'm gonna whip your butt!" "Drop him Jake!" yelled one of his buddies.

Reacting more out of anger than good sense Robbie got his fists up. Anger had replaced any sense of the weight difference or the poor odds. He had been insulted and bullied and he wasn't going to ake it anymore. Anger also caused him to forget hat he wasn't a particularly good boxer and that Jake was not only bigger but a much more experienced fighter. Jake then faked a punch with his left hand and swung another roundhouse right which connected at the same spot on Robbie's jaw. Robbie literally "saw stars." Later he would describe briefly seeing little red and yellow "stars" on a black background.

Somehow he didn't fall down. Staggering, he caught his balance again a few feet from Jake who had an evil grin on his face. He was clearly enjoying himself. Just then, Robbie had a flash of realization. "What am I doing," he thought, "I've been learning how to wrestle all winter and yet I'm trying to trade punches with this ape." Jake, if nothing else, had a killer instinct and moved back in to finish off Robbie. As Jake stepped back in for another punch, Robbie got his fists back up, but with a different strategy in mind. Jake twisted his upper body and threw another hard right hand at Robbie's jaw. This time, though, Robbie lowered his level and shot a 'double-leg' takedown under the swinging fist. Jake ended up swinging at thin air and thus was leaning forward off-balance as Robbie's shoulder slammed into his thighs.

Off-balance, Jake went down fast and hard and Robbie was on him like a cat. "Get him, Robbie!" yelled Matt. The takedown threw Jake onto his back and Robbie pounced on him, straddling his body with a knee on each side. Robbie rained lefts and rights down on Jake's head. Robbie could still feel his jaw throbbing from Jake's blows and was thirsty for revenge. He couldn't hit nearly as hard as Jake but he was certainly putting a hurt on the big bully. Jake quickly realized the futility of trying to punch up at Robbie and rolled over to his stomach. All the while, Robbie was peppering the left and right sides of his head. From his stomach Jake attempted to push up to his knees from which he hoped to grab Robbie and then kick his butt.

Robbie realized that he wasn't strong enough to hold Jake down and had a natural fear of him getting back up and pounding him senseless. At that point Robbie borrowed a technique learned from his teammate Justin and threw a leg ride in on Jake. Hooking his legs in on Jake and then throwing his weight into him caused him to fall back down to his stomach with an audible grunt The leg ride also kept Robbie's hands free and he continued to flail away at Jake. "I give up! I give up!" yelled Jake with his face down in the dirt. Robbie could still feel the pain in his jaw from Jake's heavy punches and his reaction was to yell back, "Like hell you do!" and continue trying to punch either side of Jake's face which he was now covering with both of his hands.

By then there was some obvious tension among the "innocent bystanders" as well, and wiser heads prevailed. "Let him go," said Matt, "I think he's had enough." Jake initially looked cowed as he picked his bruised face up out of the dirt but by the time he stood up he was at least faking his usual bravado.

"You better watch out Renfro!"" he said, "You cheated me with that cheap shot but I'll get you next time. You just wait!" Robbie and his friends retrieved their wet ball from the creek and headed back to the Cherokee. Jake and his buddies walked over to the water fountain to clean Jake up, frequently cursing at the other four over their shoulders. As Matt cranked up the Cherokee he coyly glanced over at Robbie and asked, "Do you still want to watch that 'Rocky' DVD, or have you ıad enough fighting for one day?" "Very funny," ·eplied Robbie, but a good laugh took some of the ension out of the air.

Chapter 24 – From Jake to Jeff

Before classes started Monday Robbie had his nose in his hall locker trying to find a textbook when someone slid up next to him. Initially he was preoccupied with trying to find his math book in the mess of his locker, but then he glanced to his left and saw Jake Armstrong eyeballing him. Robbie's pulse quickened noticeably as he remembered Jake's words at the park Sunday, "I'll get you next time. You just wait!" Robbie had been hoping for a **much** longer wait.

The expression on Jake's face confused Robbie. It was not his usual cocky look, or the angry look he had seen the day before. Jake looked as though he was a bit confused himself. "Hey, come over here outta the hall," said Jake as he stepped into an alcove leading into a classroom. Staying out in the hallway with witnesses seemed the safer path for Robbie and he stayed put. Jake shook his head and held his palms up saying, "I'm not messin' with ya, man. I just wanna talk but not out there where everybody's watchin'!" Robbie noticed for the first time that neither of Jake's cronies were with him, and for once he wasn't putting on his usual "tough guy" act. He stepped into the alcove with Jake.

It was a small alcove and the bigger Jake was taking up most of the limited space. Looking mostly down at his feet Jake began, "Robbie, you and me never really had any problems until lately. I didn't like that Floyd dude's black power poster and that got me steamed, but heck, I didn't even know you knew the dude at first. Anyway, like I said, I never had nothin' against you and I'd just as soon call things even." Initially, Robbie was stunned to see this apparently sensible side of Jake and didn't know what to say. Then he spoke up, "So you're saying you're not going to be giving me a hard time anymore, or Floyd either?" Jake replied, "Heck,

I've gotta go outa my way to even run into the guy. Now like I said, we'll just call things even." That seemed fair enough and Robbie extended his hand out for a handshake. Momentarily Jake just stared at the hand as if he was unfamiliar with displays of character. Then Jake reached out and they shook on it. "Not friends," thought Robbie, "but at least not enemies."

Later in the day, Robbie walked through the gym lobby on his way to lunch. Coach Destin was talking to the basketball coach when he spied Robbie and called him over to his office. He followed the Coach under the "Wrestling Spoken Here" sign into his office where Destin said, "Words out that you and Jake Armstrong got into it down at the park over the weekend. Let me say two things about that. First of all, fighting just about never solves anything and often makes things worse. Second of all, we don't want another situation like Floyd got into which could get you suspended and out of the Conference Tournament. In other words, keep that neighborhood problem out of the schoolhouse. If you're being threatened let me know and I'll 'go to bat' with the school administration for you."

"Wow, word travels fast," thought Robbie. He then said, "Coach, you wouldn't believe it, but Jake came up to me this morning and all but apologized. It's a truce anyway. He said he wouldn't mess with Floyd or me anymore and we shook on it." "Well, will miracles never cease!" responded Coach Destin. "Maybe Jake's showing some good common sense for once, or maybe it's because most bullies don't understand anything but brute force, sad to say. Well, I'm glad you boys got things worked out and you can concentrate on getting ready for the tournament Saturday. If trouble gets stirred up again, let me know." "Thanks coach," said Robbie and he headed down the hall to lunch.

At lunch Robbie sat down with Floyd and Matt as usual. By then word about the fight was common knowledge and a few of the other guys crowded around their table wanting to hear all the details. Robbie was embarrassed by the attention and had mixed emotions about the whole thing. His parents and teachers had always told him to try and avoid fights, but on the other hand he was glad to have come out on top in the conflict. Robbie didn't have to say much since Floyd and Matt were more than happy to fill in the specifics. "You shoulda seen it," Floyd was saying, "We thought Jake was about to crush Robbie right in the head again and then Robbie lowers his level and hits this sweet 'double-leg' right under the guy." "Right," added Matt, "You've never seen a guy more surprised than Jake as the dirt was coming up to meet his face!"

"Wait 'till Justin hears about the way you tied him up with that 'leg ride,'" said Floyd, and on they went.

By Tuesday things were closer to normal, without the fight on everybody's mind. Robbie was glad to put it all behind him, and his jaw was a lot less sore. Coach Destin reminded the team that they all knew by now which moves and holds they scored with most consistently and should concentrate on those high percentage techniques this week. "That's right," added Coach Moore, "you don't need 27 different moves to win a match. You need at least a move each from top, bottom, and standing that you're confident in." Robbie still didn't have a lot of different moves, but he knew which three he had confidence in.

During announcements at the end of practice, Coach Destin mentioned that he'd heard some of the athletes talking about their likely "seed" in the tournament and wanted to remind them not to get hung up on their seed, which would be determined based on their conference records. “Always take ‘em one at a time,” he said. “Don’t be overconfident because you’re the higher seed, that’s how upsets happen. And don’t feel that you can’t beat someone seeded higher than you. The outcome of athletic contests always comes down to three things,” he said. “How good they are, how good you are, and who’s ready to go! If you are always ready to go hard, you will sometimes knock off that favored opponent.” A lot of heads nodded in the room. Terrance spoke up saying, “That’s right Coach!”

“That reminds me of one of our former wrestlers, Marvin Brinson,” said the Coach. This time Robbie elbowed Matt, smiling and whispered “Story time.” “You’re catching on,” Matt replied. “Going into the Regionals one year,” continued

Destin, "Marvin had lost to an Ironwood wrestler three times in a row. Twice during the regular season and once in the Conference Tournament. Some wrestlers would have been 'psyched out' by then, believing that they just couldn't beat the guy. That's not the way Marvin looked at it. Really, Marvin was mad at the guy for beating him three times and wanted to get him back! When the match started the Ironwood wrestler was probably a little overconfident since he'd really handled Marvin pretty easily in their previous run-ins, but Marvin was on him like white on rice and really took it to him. This confused the Ironwood H.S. wrestler and he never really got his head back together. Marvin won by several points and placed in the Regional. So if you're the underdog Saturday, wrestle like Marvin and give it all you've got."

Wednesday in English class Mr. Long was reviewing some of the readings they had been doing in the Literature book. He opened his book and read to them a passage from Homer's The Iliad, "The two men strode out into the circle, and grappled each other in the hook of their heavy arms. Their backs creaked under stress of violent hands that tugged them stubbornly, and the sweat broke out, and raw places all along their ribs and their shoulders broke out bright red with blood, as both of them kept up their hard efforts for success and the prize."

"Robbie," said Mr. Long, "you've read the whole passage. From what you've read and your wrestling experience could you tell us what wrestling move Odysseus throws Ajax with." "Well," Robbie answered sheepishly, "it would probably be easier just to show it, without throwing anybody on the floor or anything." "Excellent," replied Mr. Long, "Choose a partner and act it out." Robbie turned to Bill in the seat behind him and said, “Let’s do it.” Bill said, “Oh no!” but got up to help. Robbie and Bill went to a clear area in the front of the classroom and Robbie explained that it sounded as though Odysseus and Ajax were both attempting "bear hugs" on each other, locked over and under the others arms. Despite Bill's reluctance they locked up and showed the likely position. “Then what Odysseus does is to trip Ajax right behind the knee.” Robbie demonstrated without throwing any weight into it…neither wanted to fall on the hard floor. “Since Ajax was straining,” continued Robbie, “when his knee got tripped from behind he lost his balance and fell on his back.”

“And thank you for that expert demonstration,” said Mr. Long who continued to say, “So you see there’s some reality involved in Homer’s stories. In fact, archaeologists have uncovered the ancient city of Troy where the Greeks were apparently at war with the Trojans as described in The Iliad."

After practice that day the "Three Musketeers" were again getting in a run when Robbie suggested they have a pull-up contest when they got back to the room. "I'm game," said Floyd. "Oh, you've been putting that Christmas present to work at home, have you?" added Matt. They gave it a shot when they got back to the room. They decided to go by weight classes so Floyd went first. Straining, he managed eleven pull-ups, much better than average. "Way to go," said Matt, "but you're goin' down!" Robbie went next and got seventeen clean pull-ups. Straining hard for number eighteen, he couldn't quite get his chin up over the bar. "You're the man," said Floyd. Robbie replied that he had worked his way up to fifteen every morning and evening now. Matt didn't look too confident but pointed to Robbie and said, "You're goin' down too, big guy." Robbie fought hard through 12, 13, 14, 15, and then got stuck halfway up on 16 before dropping to the floor. "Man!" he said, "Look's like I've got a better shot at the title Saturday night."

The week seemed to be flying by with all the athletes looking forward to Saturday's tournament. Robbie walked into the room for practice Friday afternoon and immediately was surprised to find Matt sitting against the wall talking to Jeff Fencik! Jeff had on his State team shorts and the purple and gold "Head Lock Café" team shirt Coach Destin had given him. "Hi Jeff," said Robbie, "To what do we owe the honor?" Jeff explained that the college team didn't have a match this weekend and his coach had given him the okay to come home for the weekend, provided he got in a workout. "Cool," said Robbie, "Are you coming to the tournament tomorrow?" "Right," said Jeff, "Destin said I could help coach some or maybe I'll be head cheerleader!"

During practice Robbie drilled some with Floyd, Matt, and Jeff at different times. Working with Jeff was like having his own personal coach since Jeff would frequently give him some pointers as they drilled their moves. Coach Destin ran the practice, switching the team from drill to drill while Coach Moore circulated through the room working individually with athletes when he perceived a potential problem. He worked specifically with Robbie on avoiding the 'fireman's carry' by using his set-ups and being careful with his tie-ups.

Jeff stuck around after practice with the "Three Musketeers" and said he needed a good workout to keep his weight down for next week. After the run they headed back to the room, and at Jeff's suggestion, each rotated through him for a short workout. For example, Jeff worked with Matt irst and had him run through each of his favorite noves while Robbie worked with Floyd and so orth. When it was Robbie's turn to work with Jeff ıe was able to pick up a few pointers and reminders, nostly things he already knew, to help him stay on ıis toes at the tournament.

Chapter 25 – The Conference Tournament

Three months into the season you would think that the short away trip to Ironwood High School would have been routine by now, but it was a mostly quiet bunch filing onto the activity bus Saturday morning. Oh, there was still a little kidding around, for example Justin popped Danny on the back of the head and then ran around the back of the bus, but it was a generally serious bunch with an air of tension. “I’m gonna kill that flea one day,” growled Danny. “Well wait ‘till the season’s over and I’ll help you,” added Charles.

Most of the wrestlers had brought small coolers or had their parents bring one. After weigh-in they hit the coolers for a snack, enough for some energy but not enough to feel sluggish later. As Coach Destin often said, “No one wants to see what he ate, twice.” Destin was down the hall somewhere with the rest of the head coaches at the “seeding” meeting deciding how the tournament would be bracketed and basically who would be wrestling who. Jeff and Coach Moore hung out with the wrestlers in the gym, many of which were lounging on the mat, talking, playing cards, or whatever.

After about an hour, Destin walked back into the gym carrying a copy of the bracket sheets for each weight class and gathered the team at the corner of one of the two Ironwood H.S. mats laid out on the gym floor. He then went down through the weight classes informing each wrestler of his "seed" and who his first-round opponent would be. Justin, as expected, was seeded first at 103 pounds and asked who his semi-final opponent would be, to which Destin answered, "Hold your horses, Justin and just take 'em one at a time. Let's concentrate on your first round match and we'll talk about the semi-finals later." Floyd was seeded second at 119, Robbie third at 130, and Matt first at 140.

"Remember," said Coach Destin, "Your weight class has been seeded based on your conference records in an effort at fairness, but who's going to win this tournament will be decided on the mat."

At each mat there was a total of four chairs, two each at opposite corners for the coaches. Destin explained that he and Jeff would take the seats for the Canady H.S. matches and Coach Moore would make sure each on-deck wrestler was ready to go. "If a problem comes up at any time today," said the Coach, "see Coach Moore or myself about it. Let us worry about it and you just concentrate on your wrestling."

The tournament got underway shortly thereafter starting with the 103-pound weight. There were eight wrestlers in each weight class which meant four first-round matches, two on each mat. Robbie was at 130, the fifth weight division so he had to wait a while. Justin, as usual, got the team off to a fast start. He quickly dispatched the number eight seed with a first period pin. Gary lost his first match but Floyd and Chris both won.

Robbie's first match was against the number six seed, the same wrestler he had defeated from East Springfield the week before. This being his first Conference Tournament, and only his third tournament event ever, Robbie was glad to start off with a match he was favored in. Prior to the match, Coach Moore tussled a little with him in the warm-up area trying to clear up the usual "butterflies" in advance. "Remember now," he said, "get your shot. Don't wait for him. Go right after him!"

"Go get him," said Jeff as Robbie stepped on the mat. "Just like in practice," advised Coach Destin. It helped to have some confidence going into the match and Robbie did just what Coach Moore had said. Soon after the whistle he popped his Spartan opponent on the head and dropped in under him for a successful 'double-leg' takedown. The takedown seemed to do two things: it added to Robbie's confidence and seemed to take a little of the wind out of his opponent's sails. Robbie dominated the match scoring with a 'cradle' in the first period, a 'roll' and near fall points in the second period, before locking up another 'cradle' for a pin in the third period. While locking up that last cradle Robbie could sense that his opponent had "gassed" and victory was at hand.

Robbie went up to sit with his folks in the bleachers for a while and drink some gatorade. They were pleased with the win and all three cheered Matt on to a solid victory shortly thereafter. Floyd and Matt joined them in the stands and Mrs. Renfro asked, "Would you boys like a drink? We've got some here in the cooler." They declined, each having just had one. Mr. Renfro spoke up and said, "I'm really proud of how you boys and the eam have done this season and I want to thank Matt and Floyd here for working with Robbie so much. t's done him a world of good." "I'm starting to nave some doubts about that now," laughed Floyd, "Robbie's starting to work me over pretty good in practice!"

Matt spoke up and said, "Look, somebody's updating the wall charts. Let's see if they've got our semi-final opponents posted." There were fourteen large bracket sheets, each on its own sheet of poster paper up on the end wall of the gym. Each checked his sheet. "I've got the guy I lost to in the Millsville match two weeks ago," said Robbie. "That's the match that you lost by one point on a late escape isn't it?" asked Matt. "That's right," replied Robbie, "I almost locked my 'cradle' on him and I let him slip out. What a bummer!" "Hey, you can beat that guy," Floyd pitched in. "In fact all three of us have a good shot at making the finals."

At the end of the first round, team scores were announced and Canady H.S. held a slight lead over Ironwood H.S. with Harris High in third place but close behind. The other five conference schools seemed already to be in a likely battle for fourth place. There was a short break before the semi-finals and Coach Destin sat the team down on the mat again for a meeting. Only a few Canady H.S. wrestlers had lost first round and he reminded them that the consolation rounds would start after the semi-finals. He pointed out that the biggest point scoring round in the tournament was always the semi-finals and that a good round would place us closer to our goal of team champions.

He then went down through the match-ups from the bracket sheets. When he got to the 189-pound bracket he reminded Charles that his opponent was the same Ironwood H.S. wrestler who had upset him in the match at Canady earlier in the season. "All right!" said Charles, "I'm not overconfident Coach, but I've been wanting to get that guy back on the mat for the last month. I swear, I'm gonna keep my butt down low this time and pin him with the same 'half nelson' I screwed up with last time!" "All right Charles, settle down," said Destin. "That's big talk. Now just be sure you put your money where your mouth is." "He's all mine Coach," Charles insisted.

The Pirates were off to another good start in the semi-finals. As Robbie's match approached, Coach Moore stuck with him and reminded him, "This is that guy you lost the close one to two weeks ago. Get him back. You're getting better and better every week, Robbie. You're strong. Get that cradle on him again, take your time and bump him over." The first match had been tied 3-3 going into the third period. Robbie had taken him down early on but had lost an escape and a takedown later in the period, gained an escape himself in the second, and then lost the match in the third on his opponent's escape. He didn't want to get 'bitten' by that Moccasin again. Revenge **was** an excellent motivator.

The Pirate faithful all cheered for Robbie as he toed the line against his Millsville opponent. On the whistle, they circled each other and traded shots without scoring. His opponent reached to tie up Robbie's head, so Robbie popped his opponent's arms up and shot a 'double-leg' underneath the outstretched arms. "Two, takedown," called out the referee. Robbie grabbed his opponent's foot and rode his opponent looking for his 'cradle' without success but at least he was holding him scoreless. Near the out-of-bounds line his opponent was able to pull Robbie's hand off of his foot and make a hard 'turn-in.' Robbie tried to follow the turn and they ended up facing each other out-of-bounds.

"One, escape," called the ref. As they walked back to center Robbie remembered being behind 3-2 to the guy at the end of the first period of their last match and was determined to not let that happen again. They both fought hard and the first period ended with Robbie up 2-1.

Robbie started down in the second period and, hoping for a 'roll,' tried a 'turn-in' on the whistle. Instead, the Moccasin chopped his arm and shoved Robbie down to his stomach. As Robbie rushed to push back up the top man caught him in an 'arm bar' and attempted to turn him to his back. Robbie spent the next forty seconds turning away from the pressure of the 'arm bar' and finally worked up to his knees and freed his arm. A battle for hand control then followed. Robbie finally got control of his opponent's wrist and hit a good 'turn-in.' The Moccasin almost snaked his way behind but Robbie's left foot was able to catch the top man's leg and he elevated him over to his back. The Millsville wrestler immediately bridged over to his stomach as the referee called, "Two, reversal." Robbie fought hard to ride his opponent but he managed a late escape and the second period ended with Robbie up 4-2.

Strategy raced through Robbie's mind as he got ready to start the third period in the top position. He knew that a reversal would allow his opponent to tie up the score, but with an escape and takedown his opponent could still win. No chance of overconfidence with just a two-point lead. Robbie went back to riding his opponent's foot and working his cross-face. His extra runs after practice were paying off. He was still going strong and could feel his opponent fading some. He was still strong in spurts, but not consistently.

With just less than a minute left, Robbie saw a good chance to run his 'cradle' and heard Coach

Moore on the sideline yelling, "Kiss his knee! Make him kiss it!" Robbie did just that and locked the cradle and then attempted to bump him over. "Do the bump, Robbie!" yelled Moore. Robbie was more careful this time in his position and worked the Moccasin over to his back. He bridged hard as the ref counted the near fall points. Robbie couldn't get that second shoulder down, but neither could his opponent break his grip. The match ended in the near fall position with Robbie the winner 7-2.

Matt, Floyd, Jeff, and both coaches huddled around Robbie as he stepped off the mat patting him on the head and back. "You turned that one around and you helped the team too," said Moore. "All right!" and "Way to go!" said Matt and Floyd. Destin caught his elbow and told Robbie, "I've always said I like your hustle. Just keep working that good technique."

Both Floyd and Matt also won in the semis. The three were sitting up in the bleachers with Robbie's parents as Charles Longstrom got ready to start his 189-pound semi-final match. Robbie's dad was talking to Floyd about how his match had gone and Robbie was thinking how unlikely a friendly conversation between the two would have been a few months ago. He hadn't heard his dad make a negative comment about race on the team or at school in some time. They were looking forward to Charles' match. He was "seeded" first despite his upset loss to this same Ironwood H.S. opponent earlier in the season. His opponent was seeded fourth due to more losses.

Charles charged his opponent on the whistle and shot a 'double-leg' almost immediately. He didn't score on the first shot because his opponent was back-pedaling so fast. He then tied up with him to prevent more backing off, and shot a successful akedown. Wasting no time, Charles attacked from he top with a vengeance first breaking him down and then fighting under his arm for a 'half nelson.' The bottom man attempted to turn away but Charles vould not be denied and turned him to his back. The Ironwood H.S. wrestler was hard to pin due to his strength, but Charles wore him down and scored he pin with about ten seconds left in the first period. Charles yelled, “Yes!” and was back up on his feet much quicker than his victim. “That’s good two ways,” Matt pointed out, “Charles just scored a bunch of points for us while keeping Ironwood H.S. scoreless.” “That’s right,” agreed Floyd.

Coach Destin sat the team down again after the semis were finished for an update. Canady was in first place by seven points, not much, over the Ironwood Tigers. Harris High was still in third place twelve points behind Ironwood, with the rest of the field farther back. Over half of the Pirate starters had advanced to the championship finals and the rest were still "alive" in the consolation rounds. All the consolation matches leading up to third place at each weight would be wrestled before the championship finals later that evening.

"We've got the lead so if we keep winning we will win the Conference Championship," said Destin. "If you've lost a match today we need you to get your head back together and fight hard for that third place medal. Every match you win in the consolations will also help the team score points toward the championship. For you guys in the finals, you've got to relax, get something to eat, but be ready to go mentally and physically once the finals start. A champion wrestler needs a little 'light switch' in his head," said Destin, "You need to be able to click that competition switch off and relax for a while and then be able to click it back on before you step into that circle tonight."

The wrestlers were all sitting in a corner of one of the mats again with Coach Destin on one knee addressing the group. “Another thing about that ‘light switch’ is if you can relax you keep from burning up all your energy during the down time at a tournament, which reminds me of J.J. Osborne, Canady High School’s first state champion.” Jeff was standing with Coach Moore, behind Coach Destin and he smiled and spoke up saying, “Story time!” The wrestlers laughed. Even Coach Destin smiled and nodded his head saying, “Jeff’s been around long enough to have heard most of these stories!”

“J.J.,” said Destin “was in the finals of the State Championship and he was so ‘pumped up’ about having a shot at the title that he just couldn’t sit still. He was a 189-pounder which is the twelfth weight and I was worried that he was going to wear himself out before his match even started, pacing back and forth and bouncing around. I kept telling him to just sit down with me and watch the matches, but the next thing you know he was back on his feet warming up again. Fortunately, he pinned his opponent in the first period. I've always wondered if he could have gone the whole six minutes after warming up for an hour and a half! Anyway," he continued, "you guys in the finals relax while you can. You'll have plenty of time to get ready later."

As the meeting broke up, Destin caught Robbie by the arm and called out, "Jeff." Jeff came over and Coach explained that in their first match Robbie had played the Ironwood H.S. wrestler's game and that he had a good shot of turning things around in the finals. He reminded Robbie about the two 'fireman's carry' takedowns he had lost in the first match and had Jeff try to lock up and look for a 'fireman's carry' while Robbie kept pushing him away or shooting under him. "You see Robbie, if you keep this guy out of the tie-up he wants for the ‘fireman’s carry’ then two good things can happen for you. One, you’ll have a chance to score with your ‘double,’ and two, if you get a lead on him he’s less likely to let you go from the top so you’ll be more likely to get your ‘roll.’” “I’ll do my best Coach,” said Robbie. “Believe in yourself,” added Jeff. Robbie nodded in agreement but it was hard to forget that he had lost to this same Tiger wrestler 7-3 just three weeks earlier.

The consolation finals were wrestled on both mats and then during a short break one of them was rolled up and the remaining Ironwood H.S. mat with a big Tiger painted in a corner was slid to the center of the gym for the championship finals. In the weights lower than Robbie’s, Gary at 112 had finished third and Chris at 125 fourth in the consolation finals. Justin at 103 and Floyd at 119 had both already won their championship finals matches to place first. Justin dominated on his way to a third period pin, while Floyd scored a minor upset with a 4-3 win. Floyd came over to wish Robbie luck. He was wearing both his gold medal and a big grin. He patted Robbie on the back and said, “Go for the gold, brother!”

As the referee blew the whistle to start Robbie’s finals match, Robbie was careful not to tie up with his Ironwood opponent and chance losing a takedown to his ‘fireman’s carry.’ He still felt he needed some contact to get rid of his usual “butterflies” so he took an almost immediate takedown shot. The shot failed but at least the “butterflies” were gone. The Tiger moved in quickly to tie Robbie up. Robbie knew he wanted to shoot under his opponent’s tie-ups but his more experienced opponent got a good grip on Robbie’s arms. Robbie struggled to push him off and nadvertently got his feet almost tangled. His opponent sensed Robbie was off-balance and mmediately shot his 'fireman's carry.' "Two, akedown," called out the referee. Robbie mmediately turned to his stomach but knew he was lown 2-0. "There goes Coach Destin's strategy!" hought Robbie.

It was still early in the period, plenty of time o roll him to his back he figured. He hit a couple 'turn-ins' and attempted a good roll but just then his opponent's coach yelled, "Cut him," and the Tiger et him go, confident he could take Robbie down again. "One, escape," called the ref. No "butterflies" now. Robbie got into a good low stance and solidly pushed off his opponent as he tried to tie up. Determined to score with another 'fireman's carry' the Tiger pushed in to tie up again. This time Robbie shoved his arms up, dropped down and scored with a perfect 'double-leg' takedown. "Two, takedown," called the referee. Robbie just couldn't hold him down and the Ironwood H.S. wrestler managed an escape and the first period ended 3-3.

Robbie started on top in the second period and again couldn't hold his opponent down. Robbie tried to capture his foot to hold him down but the Tiger was fast enough to stand up before he could grab it. Robbie tripped him on his first few attempts but the Tiger finally got good hand control and escaped. "One, escape," called out the ref. The two exchanged shots from their feet unsuccessfully and the second period ended with Ironwood winning 4-3.

Robbie started down in the third period. He could hear Coach Destin call from the corner saying, "He won't 'cut' you Robbie!" Coach was figuring that the top man wouldn't let him go because to do so would tie up the match.

Potentially, Ironwood could win the match by simply riding Robbie out. A ‘turn-in’ and ‘roll’ was what Robbie had in mind but his opponent was tough and broke him down to his stomach. He got back up, tried another ‘roll’ which didn’t work, tried a ‘switch’ and got countered, and hit another ‘turn-in’ which his opponent followed out-of-bounds. The referee blew his whistle.

As Robbie returned to the center he could see two things: there were fifty-five seconds left on the clock, and his opponent was breathing a lot harder than he was. That realization steeled his resolve and he fought hard for another ‘roll’ finally catching his opponent who was following just a little too slowly and elevated him over to his back. His opponent grunted with effort and immediately bridged over to his stomach. The referee called out, “Two, reversal.” Robbie **still** couldn’t hold his opponent down and he soon escaped to knot the score at 5-5.

Thirty seconds were remaining and the Tiger pressed the attack knowing a takedown would win him the conference championship. Robbie knew what to expect from this opponent now, and in better physical condition was still down in his good defensive stance. He anticipated his opponent's tie-up, shoved his arms up, and again penetrated with a deep 'double-leg' attack. "Two, takedown," called out the ref. The Tiger slapped the mat in frustration and was a beaten man. Robbie rode him out the few remaining seconds for a 7-5 victory.

Robbie got up, shook hands with his opponent, had his arm raised, and then ran to the corner of the mat and jumped up into Coach Destin's arms giving the man a big hug. "Congratulations champ," said the Coach. Soon, and with gold medals around their necks, both Floyd and Robbie wished Matt good luck. Matt didn't need the luck, and with workmanlike precision wrestled his way to his first conference championship.

Danny later lost in his finals rematch with Meatball but Terrance and Charles also won individual championships. The competition was tough and the team scores close throughout, but the Canady H.S. Pirates powered their way to the Conference Tournament Championship. As the mats were being rolled up and the bleachers pushed in Coach Destin was finishing his final announcement. “Once a champion, always a champion,” he was saying. “The type of character and hard work you’ve shown to earn this championship will help you continue to be successful throughout your life.” Mrs. Longstrom was standing close by with her digital camera and reminded him, “Let’s not forget to get a couple pictures of the conference champs!” She had no trouble getting the wrestlers to smile for the picture.

Robbie gave both of his parents a big hug and asked his dad to wear his first gold medal home. His father said, “I’d be proud to. Win or lose we’re both proud of you.”

The End

Made in the USA
Lexington, KY
19 August 2014